P9-CQQ-321

May 2010

Early Praise for *Personality Not Included*

"Wow. I devoured *Personality Not Included,* frequently shouting 'yes!' as I followed Rohit's spot-on analysis of a fundamental truth: being faceless doesn't work anymore. Personality in both people and companies is what customers get passionate about and drives seemingly unlimited success. This is one of those rare books to purchase by the case so you can give copies to employees and investors. But make sure to keep a few for yourself to read and reread so you don't miss a thing. Bravo!"

—David Meerman Scott, bestselling author of *The New Rules of Marketing and PR*

"*Personality Not Included* breaks down the old barriers between marketing, advertising, and PR and shows people how to nail the single objective of it all: creating powerful conversations with your customers and getting them to choose you over the rest."

—Timothy Ferriss, top blogger and #1 *New York Times* bestselling author of
The 4-Hour Workweek

"There are two types of small business owners—ones who know they are in the business of marketing and those who don't. For either, *Personality Not Included* is an eye-opening look at what really matters when it comes to delighting your customers. If you want a guide to being more than ordinary, get this book."

—John Jantsch, award-winning blogger and author of *Duct Tape Marketing*

"Just being pretty isn't enough anymore, today a brand also needs a strong personality to survive. In *PNI*, Rohit gives you the techniques and tools to help your brand go from wallflower to social butterfly."

—Laura Ries, bestselling author of *22 Immutable Laws of Branding,* and
cofounder of Ries & Ries

"Finally. The road map to marketing in the era of social media, which we've all so desperately needed. With *Personality Not Included,* Rohit defines the power of brand personality in a world of instantaneous, ubiquitous storytelling *and* gives marketers the practical knowledge and tools they need to transform their brands and marketing approaches with the secret weapon of personality. If there is one book I recommend every client and every agency person read right now, it's *Personality Not Included*. Every chapter gives you new ways to navigate an increasingly complex marketing landscape with clarity, nimbleness, and pragmatism. Invest in reading it—the dividends will be enormous for your brand and your business."

—Carla Hendra, chairman, Ogilvy New York and co-chief executive officer,
Ogilvy North America

Continued on next page

"Authenticity in products and personality is the new hallmark of corporate success—Rohit shows us why the days of faceless corporate spin are over and points us in an exciting new direction."

—Lucas Conley, *Fast Company* writer and author of *Obsessive Branding Disorder: The Business of Illusion and the Illusion of Business*

"No one talks about boring brands. With bountiful ideas and insights, Rohit Bhargava deftly explains how to present a brand's personality in a way that will get people talking and believing."

—Jackie Huba, coauthor of *Citizen Marketers* and *Creating Customer Evangelists*

"The secret to free marketing: give people a reason to talk about you. How? Have a personality. This fantastic book will teach you."

—Andy Sernovitz, *Word of Mouth Marketing: How Smart Companies Get People Talking*

"Filled with powerful insights, yet written like a collection of stories—you don't see many business books that are this tough to put down. If you believe that great marketing is about creating powerful experiences, then you need to get *Personality Not Included*. Rohit goes beyond how to effectively engage the customer and explains how to continue an intelligent dialogue with the customer after a brand already has their attention. The brands that learn from this book will be the ones kept from being thrown into the wastebasket of commoditization. Read this book—then read it again—it's that good!"

—Erik Hauser, founder, Experiential Marketing Forum; director, International Experiential Marketing Association; founder and executive creative director, Swivel Media

"Generation Y demands both authenticity and personality in a brand. It's why brands like Apple and Adidas continue to top lists of brands young people trust and respect even in an increasingly crowded media landscape where everyone is vying for young people's attention and loyalty. *Personality Not Included* acknowledges the real challenges for brands created by social media while reminding us that it's 'personality' that ultimately inspires your customers to not just like you, but to truly LOVE you. Rohit goes beyond the theoretical and includes lots of company stories as well as practical advice on how to bring out your brand's personality. As a blogger who has built a brand based on personality, I found Rohit's book to be an essential addition to my library."

—Anastasia Goodstein, founder, Ypulse.com and author of *Totally Wired: What Teens and Tweens Are Really Doing Online*

*Personality
<u>not</u> included

*Why Companies Lose Their Authenticity —
And How
Great Brands
Get it Back

Rohit Bhargava

New York   Chicago   San Francisco   Lisbon   London
Madrid   Mexico City   Milan   New Delhi   San Juan   Seoul
Singapore   Sydney   Toronto

1 2 3 4 5 6 7 8 9 0   DOC/DOC 0 9 8

ISBN: 978-0-07-154521-1
MHID: 0-07-154521-2

This publication is designed to provide accurate and authoritative information in regard to the subject matter covered. It is sold with the understanding that neither the author nor the publisher is engaged in rendering legal, accounting, or other professional service. If legal advice or other expert assistance is required, the services of a competent professional person should be sought.

—*From a Declaration of Principles jointly adopted by a Committee*
of the American Bar Association and a Committee of Publishers

Library of Congress Cataloging-in-Publication Data
Bhargava, Rohit.
    Personality not included : why companies lose their authenticity and how great brands get it back / by Rohit Bhargava.
       p. cm.
    Includes index.
    ISBN 978-0-07-154521-1 (alk. paper)
    1. Branding (Marketing) 2. Authenticity (Philosophy) I. Title.
    HF5415.1255.B47 2008
    658.8′27—dc22   2008008582

Read a secret alternate introduction to this book online at:
www.personalitynotincluded.com/alternateintro

McGraw-Hill books are available at special quantity discounts to use as premiums and sales promotions, or for use in corporate training programs. Special reprints of *PNI* with custom bonus content from the author are also available. To contact a representative please visit the Contact Us pages at www.mhprofessional.com.

No chickens were harmed in the writing, printing, or distribution of this book.

For my two little personalities, Rohan and Jaiden
and
to Chhavi, my accomplice in raising them.

Contents

PART TWO

Foreword

My mantra (as opposed to mission statement) is "empower people," and part of my day job is listening to people's ideas for new business. There are two big things I wish every entrepreneur knew. The first is that creating an "insanely great" product or service is a necessity. Without this, entrepreneurship is difficult, if not impossible. With it, you have a fighting chance, which is more than most companies have.

But what if your great product is competing with someone else's great product? Sometimes, having a great product is only the first step. *Personality Not Included* is about the second thing that every entrepreneur should know: Your company/product/service must have a personality.

Rohit's mantra is "personality matters." It matters for what products or services people buy, and how many others they tell about them. It matters because it can help get the best out of a team of employees. And it matters because it humanizes your brand and your products. This book explains the what, how, and why of brand personality.

If that isn't enough, here are three real-world reasons why you need to read this book:

- **Personality is the über-trend.** The Long Tail can get pretty tiring when it comes to books. For every niche marketing book about a specific subtopic of marketing, the amount of reading you need to do to keep up keeps growing. Thankfully, personality is an über-trend— one that is important to almost every business.
- **PNI is low on bullshiitake.** If, like me, you've read or skimmed dozens of business books you know bullshiitake when you smell it. Instead of focusing on theory, *PNI* has hundreds of examples, real stories, and a readable style.

- **People have tested *PNI*'s ideas.** This book is about ideas that work because they have worked for businesses already. And it doesn't hurt that Rohit's experience comes from working on building hundreds of brands instead of a single success story.

Beginning with the über example of uber examples, Apple, building brand personality has been a big part of my career. To a large degree, it was unwritten because no one had quite found a way to speak or write tangibly about its importance. Now you're holding the solution in your hands. Take the lessons here and apply them to your business. Find a way to humanize your brand, use your personality, and take your brand from good to great. The first step is to believe that personality matters. The second is to read this book.

Guy Kawasaki
Garage Technology Ventures
January 2008

Note to the Reader
The Nonobvious Way to Read This Book

Wet hair. Lather. Rinse.

—Directions on bottles of shampoo

You don't need me to tell you to start at page one and read until the end. That would be the obvious way to read this book—and if you choose to read it like that, you won't be disappointed. The nonobvious way, however, is what makes this book different.

The "formula" for most business books is to present a big idea, which is usually revealed in dramatic fashion by Chapter 3. The rest of the book offers further proof. The problem with this approach is that usually by Chapter 6, you get it. I have more than 100 marketing and business books on my shelf, and in most of them Chapter 6 is the sweet spot. Pick up your favorite marketing or business book and flip to Chapter 6; you'll see what I mean.

After that chapter, even great books often become repetitive. How many marketing books have you read cover to cover? It's not that they aren't good; it's just that after a certain amount of explanation, you understand the concept. The challenge you are usually left to figure out is how to apply it to your business.

If *Personality Not Included* were that type of book, there would probably be 12 chapters (or more). As you might have noticed by now, there are only six. Instead of those last few chapters where I could have tried to prove to you with different words how personality matters and why your organization needs one, I've added techniques, guides, and tools focused on helping you create a realistic plan for putting the theory of this book into action.

The best way to read the book is entirely up to you. You can flip between Part One and Part Two, read the book in the order in which it was written, or just skip directly to the sections that you find are the most useful at any particular time.

As an extension of the book, you can also see a full library of examples, Internet links, and extended research materials that went into the preparation of the book, at www.personalitynotincluded.com. Personality is a living thing and this site will reflect that reality over time and with a speed that is regrettably still impossible in a printed book.

You now have to decide what image you want for your brand. Image means personality. Products, like people, have personalities, and they can make or break them in the marketplace.

—David Ogilvy

Introduction

In 2005, Apple was about to introduce a product that everyone thought was too small to succeed. Coming off the phenomenal success of the first iPod launches back in early 2000, Apple's marketing team was working on promotions for what was going to be the smallest iPod yet—the new iPod Shuffle. Shaped like a stick of chewing gum and targeted at the music lover on the go (or gadget hound), the Shuffle was the smallest MP3 player ever created. After defining the portable MP3 player market with the iPod and its scroll wheel interface, this newest iPod broke with convention again by removing the screen altogether. Judging from the reviews from early testers—concluding that consumers would never buy an iPod without a screen—it was clear the marketing for this little product had to be different.

The most important and talked about feature of the Shuffle was its size. It was probably going to be too small for some people. So, in the first shipment of iPod Shuffles in the United States, attentive enthusiasts were surprised to find a hidden four-word joke at the bottom of the instructions shipped with the Shuffle: "Do Not Eat iPod."[1]

Word spread as Apple enthusiasts who purchased the product told others about it. Soon a debate raged online about whether it was a joke or a real disclaimer required by Apple's lawyers (not a far-fetched idea if you have ever had to deal with Apple's lawyers). Blogs featured images of the packaging. International consumers talked about why Apple had chosen not to include the line on packaging for the product in their country. Those four words got people talking about the product in an unexpected way.

[1] Published as "Do Not Chew iPod" in the UK. Apparently, people in the UK are already smart enough not to eat it.

Usually the disclaimer is the one part of marketing language that seems untouchable. Yet for the Shuffle, an unexpected product with a game-changing interface, the tag fit. It was a small demonstration of the personality of the product, and a reflection of the entire personality of Apple.

The sad truth is that most companies today would never allow this type of moment of personality to happen. Blame endless legal reviews or a corporate culture of fear if you like (we'll talk more about these barriers later in the book), but whatever the reason, most companies are adept at removing any sense of individuality or human connection from how they communicate. We commonly describe these companies as faceless. They are large inhuman blobs that do not listen or ask for our feedback, have incomprehensible policies, and use automated responses instead of real people to address our concerns.

These faceless organizations are all around us. As consumers, we can spot them right away, and we universally dread our interactions with them. Think about the last time you had to endure a 10-minute series of robotic questions from an automated call center in order to speak to a real person. There are dozens of videos on YouTube of customers who tried to cancel their service and couldn't, spent hours on hold, or were somehow otherwise treated like a number instead of a person. The media loves to tell these tales of corporate stupidity too, publishing them with headlines like "Woman Gets 300-Page Bill for iPhone" (a real headline from a *USA Today* article in August 2007).

Personality Matters

Clearly, being faceless doesn't work anymore. The problem is that many organizations today are stuck dealing with their customers, partners, and employees in a faceless way. Some don't realize it and others are too paralyzed to change. The biggest challenge most organizations today face is discovering how to go from a brand that people consume to one that they are passionate about. Every company has a different solution to this challenge, from focusing on product design and innovation to renewing focus on better branding in order to better tell the story of a product or service.

The theory of *Personality Not Included* is that personality is the answer. Personality is the key element behind your brand and what it stands for, and the story that your products tell to your customers. Every element of your business, from your interactions with your customers to the packaging of your product is an element of your brand personality, and these are the elements that inspire delight or indifference among your customers. In short, *personality matters*.

Of course, just telling you that doesn't make it true, so read on to learn more about what I mean by personality, what the elements are, and how you can tackle the most difficult question of all: how can you find a way to inject personality into your brand when the majority of marketing conventions today focus on helping you shield your personality from the world? The first step is changing your perception of what marketing can or should do.

Marketing Is Not about Selling

Apple's disclaimer may have been a small element in a sea of marketing, but it manifested an identity that consumers already associated with the Apple brand. The disclaimer was irreverent, different, and nontraditional, just like Apple. The power of Apple's brand is about more than putting out innovative products. Speak to any Apple enthusiast and you will understand that the real reason Apple succeeds is that it is telling a story that its customers get passionate about, and, more important, tell others about. The real genius of Steve Jobs's legendary keynote product announcements is how the announcement itself whips Apple's most vocal customers into a frenzy deep enough to tell everyone else they know about Apple's new products.

What Apple knows about great marketing is that it is about more than selling. Selling will usually take care of itself if you have something decent to sell at a reasonable price. If you want to create marketing focused on selling, all you need to do is answer four simple questions for your consumer:

1. **Features.** What does your product do for me and why is it different and/or better than others?
2. **Benefits.** How will my life be different/better/changed if I purchase it?
3. **Price.** Why it is worth what you are charging?
4. **Action.** Where can I get it?

If you consistently provide good answers to these questions with your marketing, I guarantee you will be able to sell whatever you are trying to sell. Of course, if it was that easy no companies would ever fail. Answering these four questions with good answers is not necessarily a simple thing, but the formula this creates for selling anything is very straightforward. The problem with focusing on only these four is what Fred Reichheld, author of *The Ultimate Question*, called "bad profits." These are the profits that you earn without keeping the customer happy. *Personality Not Included* is for marketing and sales professionals who believe that marketing needs to do more than generate this type of profit. It is for companies that want to be *loved* instead of liked. It is for organizations that want to be iconic instead of ordinary.

Every company that consumers are passionate about already understands that sharing an authentic identity inspires loyalty and belief. If you're a fan of playing "buzzword bingo," then congratulations on your first hit.[2] Buzzword bingo is a Dilbert-esque way of drawing attention to overhyped buzzwords as they are unleashed in conversation by yelling "bingo" to cause extreme embarrassment for the offending buzzword user. And since *authenticity* is most definitely a buzzword, you can go ahead and yell "BINGO!" now.

Luckily, this is not just a book about being more authentic (or about how to play buzzword bingo). Authenticity is part of the story, but it is only one element of something bigger and not an end goal in itself as many people may be tempted to assume today. I do want to help you make your business more authentic, but focusing on that alone is not enough. Your customers *want* to believe in an authentic brand, but they need the right incentive. *Personality is that incentive.*

Defining Personality

Personality is a loaded term today, which for many conjures up images of endless multiple-choice questions leading up to a formulaic four-letter description of your personality. For years, it was these tests that defined how we thought about personality. Raise your hand if you are an ENFP.[3] Those types of tests have their uses, but to think about personality within marketing, we need a new definition for personality—one that goes beyond scientific scoring methods or quick answers to online surveys.

A search on Amazon.com will yield dozens of books dedicated to helping you understand your personality so you can achieve spiritual oneness, find your perfect mate, understand your work colleagues better, or be a better parent. Understanding personality seems to be the key to emotional intelligence.

---

[2] If you are unfamiliar with this game, visit http://www.personalitynotincluded.com/bingo to download a custom version.

[3] ENFP is my Meyers-Briggs personality score. Your results may vary.

This book is not about emotional intelligence. It's not that I don't care about you achieving a spiritual understanding of yourself. I'm Indian and all for that (and good luck with your journey, by the way). But the big idea of *my* book is that personality is the key to creating an inspiring brand.

Personality is the unique, authentic, and talkable soul of your brand that people can get passionate about.

Personality is not just about what you stand for, but how you choose to communicate it. It is also the way to reconnect your customers, partners, employees, and influencers to the soul of your brand in the new social media era.

Wait, Is This Really an Era?

If calling where we are now an era seems like a stretch to you, let's try an experiment. Without going online or asking someone smart: define an era. If you agree with the current definition on Wikipedia, an era is a "long period of time." Okay, sounds pretty simple. Now name an era from the past 500 years. Any one will do.

Did you come up with any? The Meiji era in Japan from 1868 to 1912 was also known as the Age of Enlightenment, during which the country embraced modernization and replaced the rule of the Samurai warriors with a representative government. In the UK, the Victorian era from 1837 to 1901 resulted in similar enlightenment during which time Darwin wrote his famous *Origin of Species*, the first World's Fair was held, and England introduced free education for all children. The point is, eras are pretty significant.

Based on these examples, I think a more complete definition for an era could be "a finite period of time during which some kind of significant enlightenment happens." That's where we are now, and the population becoming "enlightened" is your consumers.

Power is shifting from businesses to individuals, and it is fundamentally changing how marketing works. When I walk into a car dealership to look at a car today, I already know the bottom price I should ask for, what the dealer's margin is, and what all the options are. When is the last time a car salesman was able to sell rust-proof coating? This empowerment through information is happening all over the world.

Farmers in Kenya are using their cell phones to check crop prices and run their businesses, saving wasted trips and even conducting banking through mobile transactions. Hollywood movies can no longer rely on a big opening weekend for a subpar movie to cover the production costs. Word is out by early Friday night. I call this the "window of suckiness" (i.e., how long a movie is able to suck before everyone knows about it), and it means a big opening weekend is no longer guaranteed. There are hundreds of ways to buy the same product today, online or offline. Along with growing access to information and increasing choices, technology is also putting consumers in control with tools like DVRs and pop-up blockers help consumers filter out marketing messages.

Enlightenment is happening right now. People are moving from simply consuming content to creating it. RSS feeds, blogs, wikis, social networks, and media online and on demand are giving people more ways than ever to control the content they choose to watch, read, or interact with. The Internet is evolving too, shaping itself around the people who access and contribute to it, rather than a directory of pages about topics. That's Web 2.0 and we all know it's here.

Consumers are enlightened because they have the power to decide what to buy, where to buy it, how much to pay for it, and what marketing messages to believe about it. They are powerful because they have the ability and desire to share their voices with others.

This is the social media era, where all forms of media are portable, personal, and filtered—where brands have fewer secrets and have their identities shaped by perception as much as communication. We are in an era, and that era means you need to think differently about how you market your products and services.

The Case for Personality

Thinking differently requires focusing less on marketing your products and benefits, and more on understanding how to use the personality behind your brand to build a relationship with your customers. Talk to any brand that has found a passionate customer base and you will see the same elements come forth. The power of personality is something that I have slowly realized over more than a decade of helping hundreds of brands of all sizes create marketing strategies that work. Every company is trying to solve the same challenge: how to stand out from its competitors and build a relationship of trust with its customers.

Whether you are a large multinational technology company or a small dental surgery practice, the power of personality is equally important. Personality inspires trust and trust builds loyalty. It is a very simple progression that most people intuitively understand. Throughout this book, you will see more than a hundred examples of companies and influential individuals who have all uncovered the power of personality as a core element of their success. You will understand how personality can often be the secret weapon driving great companies to build the kind of customer loyalty their competitors envy. To do that, we need to first become comfortable with what could be the most dangerous word in marketing: truth.

Finding Your Yoga

Truth is a loaded word. Marketing is not about the search for truth, and we all know it. If it were, no one would believe that a bottle of water shipped halfway across the world with an image of a Swiss mountain on it was any more healthy than one bottled in a Coca-Cola plant in Connecticut. To compensate for having a less than interesting "truth" behind their products, brands often invent a truth. If I told you the number of times I have been in meetings where people debated whether we should use the word *healthful* or *healthy* to describe a product, you'd understand the pain involved in trying to find a truth. Maybe you feel it already.

The truth behind your product is not the terms you are legally allowed to use. Instead, truth is something deeper. In a manifesto written for the Web site ChangeThis.com, Piers Fawkes and Simon King, authors of the popular marketing blog PSFK.com, shared the idea of finding your "yoga." Yoga, they wrote, was "the truth which people want to see, stripped to the core. If you are going to tell the truth, then you have to be sure that at the centre of your brand there is a bit of Yoga going on (and that it's the truth)."[4]

In the context of their manifesto, yoga was what brands should aim for, the ultimate truth of your product or service that you share with the world. Of course, businesses tend not to do well when it comes to telling the truth. It is part of the reason why storytelling is such a popular concept in marketing today. Indeed, marketing guru Seth Godin famously titled his book on the necessity for marketers to tell stories *All Marketers Are Liars*. Of course, he used the title to entice you to open and buy the book,

---

[4] ChangeThis Manifesto—Is Truth the Next Big Truth? (http://www.changethis.com/13.Truth)

but it raises an important point. All marketers *do* need to create a story that consumers can believe and associate with based on their view of the world. And in their quest to do so, marketers often stretch the truth.

Part of the power of personality is that it can help you bring your marketing closer to the truth, because it requires you to rely on many messengers to tell your story for you. It is nearly impossible to continue in a lie, no matter how well crafted, when you are relying on others to spread the message for you.

Bad Ideas Don't Get Better with Personality

You will find a lot of ideas in this book for how personality can be used to reinvent your marketing and how your customers perceive and relate to you. Before getting too deep into these ideas, I should probably let you

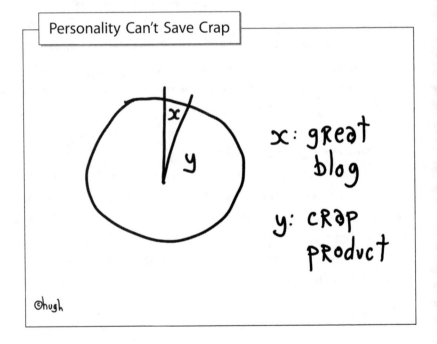

know the one thing *personality* can't do for you. Personality can't turn a bad idea into gold, and it can't compensate for a product or service no one wants. This is not a book about how to create a great product or find the right business to start. There are several insightful books on this topic that I highly recommend, including Guy Kawasaki's *Art of the Start* and *Blue Ocean Strategy* by W. Chan Kim and Renée Mauborgne.

Each will help you to craft a product or service that stands apart, has a strong business reason for existing, and has a unique value. Guy's suite of great books on the subject will even teach you the all-important job of getting your revolutionary idea funded. The job of marketing should not be to trick unsuspecting customers by creating a false need or promoting a substandard product.

By picking up *PNI*, I suspect you believe that your product or service is more than a pig in need of a makeover. This is where most businesses are: they have something marketable, but have trouble taking the next step. As a result, they are under constant threat from competitors and struggle to maintain their slight success.

Whether you have a new idea that you believe will change an entire industry, or are stuck in a commodity business where you are forced to compete on price, the lessons in this book are all about helping your business stand out. Personality is the reason consumers love one product more than another. It is what sets great companies apart and it is about more than having a game-changing product. If every product you plan to launch is the next iPhone, then you have a great head start. But that is not a necessity. Personality can help you go from good to great.

Why You Need This Book

The question you need to ask yourself is what do you want your marketing to do? If you are like most businesses, you want your marketing to tell people who you are and inspire them to buy whatever you are selling. It's that simple. I mentioned how marketing is not about selling but about building a relationship. The traditional way to look at marketing is by the four Ps. If you have ever taken a marketing course, gone to business school, or met someone who has, you will know these well. Product, price, promotion, and place were seen for decades as the core elements of all marketing. Guess what I think the fifth "P" should be?

Personality is the missing ingredient keeping most organizations from becoming great. The real reasons that you should read this book are not only so that you can outpace your competitors (you can), make more money than them (you should), or inspire your customers to be more passionate about your brand (they will be). Those are the reasons you would read any business book, aren't they?

There are four simple things that set *PNI* apart.

1. **Personality is *the* macro trend.** The three hottest topics in business today are how to do more with social media (blogs, social networks, etc.), using word-of-mouth marketing (the number one source of influence according to just about every international study), and interacting more authentically with customers. Personality is the theme that incorporates all of these topics.

2. **I still have a day job.** I work at one of the biggest marketing agencies in the world, with a client list that includes some of the world's largest and fastest-growing brands. When companies work with us, they buy time from people like me. People who lead the strategy meetings and actually figure out what to do.

I am not a professional theorist. Every idea in this book is one that I am using for real clients to get real results every day.

3. **Stories, stories, and more stories.** As you read, you will notice that there are lots of company stories. Throughout the book there are more than 100 examples of people, organizations, or products that are using personality in some way to market a product. Just about every point is made with a company as an example, in order to bring the ideas to life and demonstrate that the idea of putting personality into your business is more than just a theory.

4. *PNI progresses from theory to action.* Giving you another book with just a big idea and leaving you on your own to implement it is not useful. I know because I've read too many books like that. For that reason, *PNI* has two parts. The first reveals the theory of personality and the second is all about putting the theory into action. I want to help you understand why personality matters, and also give you the tools and action plans to use it immediately in your business.

Inside Part One: The Theory

To take you inside the book in more detail, here is an overview of what you will learn in each chapter and section.

The first section is all about personality and its role in marketing. Consider this part the theory.

Chapter 1 delves into how being faceless used to work and how it led many organizations to make choices designed to hide their authenticity and identity from their customers. It also addresses the common myth that only large companies are faceless and introduce the real secret to building a personality that most companies don't know.

Chapter 2 looks at how social media is fundamentally changing the way that organizations communicate. I introduce the idea of "accidental spokespeople" and how they are often the unofficial voices that are reinventing how consumers view companies and brands. You will learn about the key types of spokespeople and how accidental spokespeople are creating an entirely new way of looking at who speaks for your brand.

Chapter 3 returns to the definition of personality introduced at the start of the book and takes you through a new framework of thinking about your brand and products called the *UAT Filter* that will help you to understand the personality of your organization and products and how to translate this into a communications strategy to drive your marketing.

Chapter 4 explores the concept of a *marketing backstory* and takes you through a range of real examples of products and companies that have crafted these backstories to great success. Going through these cases, you will learn all the elements of a good backstory and a process for creating yours based on the little-known techniques that screenwriters in Hollywood pioneered and still use today to create a compelling story line.

Chapter 5 talks about the common situation every ambitious person is likely to encounter at least once no matter where he or she works: the roadblocks. Drawing on case studies of people who have managed to overcome personal and organizational resistance, this section will teach you how to navigate the roadblocks that prevent us from using personality, obstacles that are created by bosses, peers, investors, and lawyers, without getting fired or flamed.

Chapter 6 (the last in Part One) introduces the idea of "personality moments" and how to recognize what these are in order to put your personality to work. Based on examples of the types of situations where personality can make a difference, this chapter will offer a guide for evaluating these moments and the right way to take advantage of them. A bridge to the second part of the book, this section will lay the framework for putting your personality into action.

Inside Part Two: The Action

In Part Two you'll find a collection of materials designed to help you take the ideas and theories from Part One and put them into action. It is divided into two key sections.

TECHNIQUES **Ideas and insights**	These are methods of marketing and new ideas that you can use to put your personality into action in order to devise new forms of marketing and communications. While these do introduce new ideas, each comes with a practical step-by-step implementation strategy that allows you to immediately put the idea into action.
GUIDES & **TOOLS** **How-tos that are** **related to each chap-** **ter in Part One**	These are a collection of guides, checklists, question forms, printable resources, sample text for ideas, and more. Essentially, these are all the practical step-by-step lessons that relate to each chapter to help you move from theory to action.

Introducing Visual Bookmarking

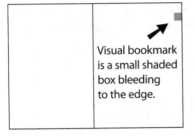

Visual bookmark is a small shaded box bleeding to the edge.

To help relate the theories in Part One to the associated action in Part Two and let you go quickly between them, this book uses an idea called visual bookmarking. The guides and tools in Part Two are organized by chapters and each chapter has a small tab on the side of the page whose vertical positioning corresponds to the guides and tools associated with that chapter in Part Two.

Getting Started

Every product and company has a personality. The problem is that businesses today have gotten extremely good at hiding it behind carefully scripted disclaimers and processes. The future of business means building real connections with customers. That future requires you to rediscover the personality of your organization and use it to bring more humanity to the way you interact with customers.

To get started, we need to take a page from the techniques of counselors who help people with all sorts of issues. The first thing they always do is get their clients to admit they have a problem. The problem with business is facelessness, and the first step is to admit that you have a problem and to recognize why it exists.

PART ONE

Chapter 1

Sign Here to Read This

How Organizations Lose Their Personality

FLETCH—Tell you what. I'll consult with my people, and they'll contact their people, who'll get in touch with your people.

BECKY—Who are your people?

FLETCH—Who are yours?

BECKY—As I told you, that has to be confidential.

FLETCH—Very well. I'll just have my people contact each other then. Have to keep them busy.

—*Fletch Lives*, 1989[1]

The moment that organizations lose their personality is when their employees become "people" rather than individuals. Most of us know this phenomenon only too well, because we have seen it happen to companies that we interact with as customers. The examples are all around us, as social media allows just about anyone to expose these moments of corporate facelessness rapidly and widely. On the Internet you can see a video

---

[1] http://www.fletchwon.net/flscript6.html

of travelers on a plane grounded on the Tarmac for seven hours (the video has been edited, thankfully). Or a video of a technician from a cable company asleep on a customer's couch during a service call. Or a lie being told to customers by a salesperson at a leading retail store as to the cost of a replacement laptop battery in order to convince them to buy a warranty.

Once upon a time, these were merely customer horror stories told among friends that would occasionally make it onto the local evening news. If there is one thing that is universally true of the Internet today, it is that there are no secrets. Isolated situations like these make it onto YouTube and generate millions of views. Company CEOs are outed for participating on message boards with pseudonyms, and it sometimes seems that no bad deed goes unblogged.

Spirit Airlines learned this the hard way in late 2007 when its CEO, Ben Baldanza, accidentally hit "Reply to all" on a response to a consumer complaint about a delayed flight instead of just sending it to his associate. His message read:

> Please respond, Pasquale, but we owe him nothing as far as I'm concerned. Let him tell the world how bad we are. He's never flown us before anyway and will be back when we save him a penny.

Of course, this e-mail hit the blogs in short order, and really took off when it was published on the blog The Consumerist, which every business should read religiously because it provides a running commentary on how being faceless doesn't work anymore. The Consumerist is one of the most popular blogs on the Internet and has become a champion for consumers everywhere who have had an experience they want to share with the world. Founded by Ben Popkin as a forum for giving a voice to consumers, the site publishes positive and negative stories about how companies interact with their consumers.

The Consumerist describes itself as a place dedicated to helping "shoppers bite back" and is the leading online destination for satisfying the desire of wronged consumers to exact their public revenge. The site is proof that the idea of a silently suffering consumer no longer exists.

The Likeability Factor

One reason this consumer-led retribution has become so popular is that it is much easier to attack a faceless company than a real person. This is a lesson that the writers of *The Simpsons* brought to life in one episode where Homer Simpson considers getting cable TV illegally after reading the following brochure:

So, You've Decided to Steal Cable

Myth: Cable piracy is wrong.

Fact: Cable companies are big, faceless corporations, which makes it okay.

This is how most people feel about faceless organizations. It seems okay to criticize an organization when it is faceless. That's what makes the video of a traveler being stuck on a Tarmac for seven hours that I mentioned earlier so powerful. Imagine if the same video unfairly criticized an overworked, underpaid, overabused stewardess nearing the end of a 14-hour shift as she struggled to keep customers calm. It wouldn't have the same effect, would it? The lesson in this is that nearly every situation in which a company is attacked by a vengeful customer is one that could have been avoided if the company had had more individuals, as opposed to people, working for it.

A key part of this is the *likeability factor*. In the medical profession, for example, one thing every doctor knows, which many marketers are still ignorant of, is that likeability matters. Statistics time and again prove that people don't sue doctors they like, regardless of how badly they screw up.

GO TO GUIDE p.239 Whether or not a customer sues a company is a similar situation to the case of doctors and their patients; it depends largely on how the company interacts with its customers. In the world of business today, many companies are not attuned to the importance of likeability. As a result, every day we still see examples like Baldanza's e-mail that demonstrate a surprising level of contempt for customers—though most may not be as blatant. In a faceless company, it's okay to hate your customers, because the excuse you can give is that you're just doing your job.

Before you can correct this, however, you need to understand why it happens. The greatest myth of facelessness is that it is just a side effect of growth. This is not true. To prove why, let's ask a question that has been asked over and over again throughout the years (though usually for different reasons).

Does Size Matter?

It is easy to believe that size matters. When a small company hires more people, invariably the new employees do not feel the same deep connection to the vision of the company that the original team may have felt. In the name of expansion, the uniqueness and enthusiasm of the original voices that started the company are lost and compromises are made. Many people believe that it is just a matter of time and size before any company becomes faceless simply because of the number of employees it has working for it. This belief is flawed, however, because it is based on a false assumption: that every company is born with a personality.

A business does not automatically have a personality because it is small. To understand this fact, let's consider the story of Jim and Alice. They've owned a convenience store in Seattle, Washington, for more than 20 years. They have a small group of regular customers, but their business is slowly eroding. The reason is predictable.

They are facing competition from a Whole Foods market down the street and a department store in the same area. Many of their customers are now ordering their groceries online. New residents have moved into the area and they have not developed any sort of bond with Jim and Alice. Local department stores now carry a wider variety of items for lower prices than Jim and Alice can afford to offer. Yet, Jim and Alice are not failing because their business is smaller. Being small can be an advantage when it comes to using personality. Jim and Alice are failing because they are not focused on using their personality to stand out. . .something they never had to do before. They survived simply because they offered convenience, but convenience is no longer enough (a point we will explore further in Chapter 3).

Now what if I told you that I made up Jim and Alice's business? That they don't exist and there is no such store in Seattle? It wouldn't matter. Their story is the same as thousands of businesses across the world that haven't realized that personality could be their greatest asset. Instead, many of these small companies simply remain ordinary, doing nothing unique or noteworthy, and therefore failing to project a special identity of any kind. We might buy from them, but we could switch tomorrow if something better comes along.

For a business of any size, one of the most important challenges is to find a way of dealing with customers that creates a real bond. The owner or staff members of a small business may speak with the same person on the phone each time that person calls, or see the same person at the checkout counter every time that person walks in; but this alone is not enough to create a strong and lasting bond. Why don't businesses in this situation do more to bond with their customers?

It seems clear that a smart business should understand the need for an authentic connection with its customers as a way to ensure they keep them as customers. Surely the one great advantage that Jim and Alice had at their disposal was the willingness to be real people and connect authentically with their customers, right? The reason they didn't is the same reason businesses of any size lose personality, which leads to a telling truth. Becoming faceless is not accidental or inevitable. It is a choice companies of all sizes make *on purpose*.

Why Being Faceless Used to Work

This is hard to believe, isn't it: that a company would choose to be faceless? Think back to the first time you heard the word "faceless." Chances are it was being used to describe a company, right? Today we recognize it as a fairly negative word, but it was not always so. To understand why any company would choose to become faceless, we need to look a bit deeper at what being faceless used to mean versus what it means today, and at the benefits that companies used to realize if they hid their identities.

GO TO GUIDE p.237

1. **Adding layers inspired consumer trust.** In the past, no one expected to reach a responsible person with power at a company directly on the phone or by just showing up at an office. The more successful the organization, the more layers you could expect to encounter between the organization and its customers. If a company did not have those layers, you might question

whether it was big enough to be trusted.

2. **Advertising defined a company's identity.** Without the ability of customers to easily share their perceptions about a company's brand with the world, as they can today, defining and projecting an identity was usually a matter of purchasing advertising placements with the right message placed in the right locations. When a company could shape consumer perceptions of its identity through controlled messages, why bother putting a real face on it?

3. **Consistency was a successful business principle.** Consistency was the core principle leading to the rise of fast food restaurants; chains of clothing, sporting goods, book, and other retailers; and department stores. The success of McDonald's, for example, is attributed in large part to the brand's ability to regulate sameness across all of the company's worldwide operations. Consistency, however, is the enemy of individuality, because if you focus solely on creating a consistent experience, your locations and employees therefore have to act the same way and institute the same policies everywhere. Today this is no longer enough.

4. **Risk management was the first priority.** Safety, in a business sense, meant protecting the company from negative situations. Allowing personnel to have individual voices or to share a real perception was dangerous for a company because it meant giving up control, which could result in lawsuits, loss of reputation, or a decrease in product sales. The decision to manage risk by removing individuals from the public eye used to be among the most critical an organization could make.

All of the above reasons point to the truth that I shared earlier: a business lacks a personality because it has made a deliberate choice to hide it. This alone, though, doesn't explain how organizations lose their personality. Here are three key factors.

1. Being ordinary (and profitable).
2. Focusing on policies rather than logic.
3. Silencing employees.

How Organizations Hide Their Personality

Looking at the list of ways personality can be lost or hidden, one thing that can be seen is that it is not an overnight process. To understand how this gradual process works, let's delve more deeply into the three elements that lead to this, starting with being ordinary.

Being Ordinary (and Profitable)

The mark of an ordinary company is that it sells products that you expect in a forgettable environment. There are millions of profitable, ordinary businesses around the world. Ordinary does not mean failing. If the company has the right products in the right place at the right time, they are going to sell. Ordinary or not, this formula works, and there is nothing wrong with it. If a company defines its business and its marketing by what it needs to do in order to be profitable, then ordinary can be good enough, for a while. Here's an example:

At the beginning of the twentieth century, the first five-and-dime stores were popping up around the United States. Deriving their name from the fact that they actually sold most of their products for between a nickel and a dime—the stores were highly popular as destinations for good products at good prices. One of the most famous of these stories was opened by Sebastian Spering Kresge in Detroit in 1899. By 1912, he owned 85 stores all named after him and was making annual sales of more than $10 million. In 1962 amid increasing competition, the new president of Kresge stores opened his first discount department store in Garden City, Michigan, and called it something different: Kmart. The store took off and by 1977 the company officially changed its name to Kmart Corporation. Kmart is the old reliable department store that has always been there. It sells ordinary products at ordinary prices, and has had a profitable business. Until Target came along, that is.

The story of Target's rise to the top in the discount department store category has been well profiled in marketing books and magazines. The story is also thoroughly chronicled by business reporter Laura Rowley in her book *On Target: How the World's Hottest Retailer Hit a Bull's-Eye.* Indeed, the "world's hottest retailer," as Rowley calls the company, well outpaced Kmart (and others) to become America's second most profitable retailer behind Wal-Mart.

Target does discount its fashion merchandise. The stores carry current fashions instead of leftovers from last year's collection. They've reinvented the way that prescription bottles appeared with their award-winning Clear Rx bottle design. The stores feature iconic products and fashions from designers that would usually only sell in more upmarket stores. All this helped them take the store from being just plain "Target" to being "Tarzhay."

What made Target such a runaway success while Kmart struggled and eventually went into Chapter 11 reorganization in 2003? Robyn Waters, then Target's VP of Trend, Design and Product Development, described Target's strategy as focused on creating the paradox of an "upscale discounter." Her focus on the power of paradoxes, which she also explores in her book, *The Hummer and the Mini* (an analysis of trends and countertrends), is an intriguing idea we will revisit later in the book as well. Target had developed an understanding of what people were buying and what affected their purchases. It was no longer enough to simply sell reasonable products for a rock-bottom price. Design mattered and style was the new currency. Kmart failed to recognize this shift and lost its position of dominance as a result.

Focusing on Policies Rather Than Logic

Airlines are the worst offenders when it comes to enforcing policies based on minimal logic. I was once bumped from a flight that had a single seat left because the airline's policy was not to assign seats within 30 minutes of departure. However, if I had called my travel agent, canceled my previous ticket, and bought a new ticket for the same seat, then the company would have let me on the flight. Who doesn't have a similarly idiotic travel story to share? Airlines and the travel industry as a whole have done a terrible job of justifying the logic of their policies.

GO TO GUIDE p. 241

Most companies feel they need policies and rules. Often, these companies are so concerned with being perceived by their customers as professional that they focus excessively on this, which kills any chance of sharing a more authentic identity. When was the last time you heard an airline flight attendant go "off script" and explain to you why the seat backs have to be in a full and upright position in order for takeoff to happen? For that matter, why is there a 20-minute wait to speak to a customer service agent at 3 a.m.? Why are accessories sold separately and batteries not included?

These brainless policies are synonymous with faceless organizations. They are usually written by lawyers or mandated by government, and are therefore devoid of personality. No authentic person could ever come up with rules like these and justify them. Can you imagine the original writer of the often-ridiculed warning tags on mattresses actually defending the necessity for them in a conversation? Logic has unfortunately taken a backseat to policy.

One problem with such policies is that consumers today are smarter than the policies account for. We all know that accessories are sold separately and batteries are not included so that a manufacturer can make more money. We know that the plane *could* take off even if those tray tables weren't stored. We assume that when we dialed a call center at 3 a.m. and were placed on hold, it was because there was just one agent on duty and not because of "high call volume."

Common sense is more pervasive than most companies might realize. The policies of many companies, however, assume that consumers are naive or stupid, for example, pointing out obvious hazards or telling customers not to do silly things, and generally giving marketers free rein to cram every undesirable message into the smallest legible font size possible. And even though cigarettes are among the most heavily regulated products in terms of required warnings, some manufacturers, when marketing brands that target males, will use tricks like talking about how smoking can be harmful for pregnant women. Policies and disclaimers are the mark of the faceless organization.

Silencing Employees

Perhaps no other trend in the marketing and communications processes of companies has been more instrumental in the loss of the personality of organizations than the "employee silencing policy." Though not usually called by this name, the policy is essentially what it says it is— a declaration that employees are not allowed to be brand or product spokespersons unless officially trained. The rationale behind this policy is usually that not every employee can be trusted to speak on behalf of a company, and that the company's PR team has a responsibility to prevent employees from speaking out of turn.

The flaw in this logic is that employees are already your brand spokespeople to a degree because they are already talking about the organization they work for in their own personal interactions. In Chapter 2, we will explore how these same employees are now sharing their voices far beyond their own personal circle of contacts as well. Despite this obvious flaw, there are three main reasons why companies established policies to silence employees and why some still stick to these policies today.

1. It is easy to replace employees when no one knows who they are.
2. Controlling messages is far simpler if you control who speaks for you.
3. The ability to be an effective spokesperson is determined by skill as a communicator rather than passion for the product or service.

One irony in the silencing of a company's employees is that sometimes the people in the best position to be authentic spokespersons and ambassadors for an organization are its employees. Compare how a message-trained communications professional describes his or her company with the way it is described by a passionate employee who has spent years developing a product and believes it is the greatest invention in the world. These are two different kinds of messages, but each has a value. Some would argue that the message of the passionate employee has the most value.

By silencing these individuals, many organizations have lost their best chance of creating authentic dialogue and of having real people demonstrate their brand's personality. As we will discuss in Chapter 2, this was a serious mistake, which is now being reversed as the rise of "accidental spokespeople" is changing what works.

Now that we know the three critical ways in which an organization can lose its personality, it will be helpful to illustrate how this has happened in a real company. And this is the perfect time to introduce every marketing book's favorite example, a company that for many years would have been considered the ultimate case study of a brand with personality—until it started to lose it. Starbucks.

The Plight of Starbucks

Do you think Starbucks is a faceless organization or a brand with a great personality? Ask 10 people you know living anywhere in the world this question and chances are you will get several disagreements. Starbucks is the ultimate brand with personality that has arguably lost it and been struggling to get it back ever since. As Howard Schultz, founder of Starbucks, realized back in 1999 when he published his book *Pour Your Heart into It:*

> The key threat to the Starbucks brand was a growing belief among customers that the company was becoming corporate, predictable, inaccessible or irrelevant. When I heard that some people viewed us as a faceless corporation, I knew I had to take a more visible role in explaining who I am and what my goals for Starbucks were. Clearly, we had not told our story well enough.

Since opening with just 11 stores in 1987, Starbucks has grown to more than 14,000 stores worldwide. Along the way the company has dealt consistently with the threat of being seen as faceless and has struggled to create a unique identity. Schultz's early solution was to offer more of a personal face to Starbucks—but that alone could not solve the problem.

In early 2007, Schultz himself realized this as he warned his colleagues about the dangers facing the Starbucks brand in a now-infamous internal e-mail leaked on the Starbucks Gossip blog. It read:

> Over the past ten years, in order to achieve the growth, development, and scale necessary to go from less than 1,000 stores to 13,000 stores and beyond, we have had to make a series of decisions that, in retrospect, have lead to the watering down of the Starbucks experience, and, what some might call the commoditization of our brand.

Pointing to business choices like replacing the manual La Marzocco espresso machines with automatic ones and no longer roasting and grinding coffee in front of customers, Schultz lamented that the trade-offs Starbucks had made for speed and efficiency were losing the "romance and theater" of the in-store coffee experience. The brand, long fueled by word of mouth, recently even started running television ads. Clearly, something is changing at Starbucks.

Still, Starbucks was founded as the "third place," away from work and home. Walking into a Starbucks anywhere in the world for the most part still carries the promise of a unique experience. This experience is not about the coffee or the music and books sold there. It cannot be exported into small glass bottles of Frappuccino sold in grocery stores. And it cannot be transmitted through a single charismatic leader (even though Schulz recently took back the reins at Starbucks to presumably lead them back to their heritage and even took the drastic step of simultaneously closing 7,100 outlets for three hours to retrain staff). The personality of Starbucks is in the destination and the group of individuals who work there. The chal-

lenge is bringing it out. The problem Starbucks is struggling ᵛ
of personality, and their example leads to an interesting revelaᵗ

The Real Secret of Personality

Imagine that you took all of the marketing that you have done or are planning to do with your brand and put it into two categories. The first category would include anything you are doing to attract new customers. This is the activity that you are aiming at people who have never purchased anything from you and who may not have heard of you. The other category would include any marketing efforts that are focused on your existing customers and your employees.

What does the ratio look like? For most companies, it looks like this:

The real secret of personality is to do the opposite. If you want to start creating an authentic bond with your customers, and stand out from your competitors, get your best ambassadors to do the work for you. In order to do that, you need to start thinking about your current customers

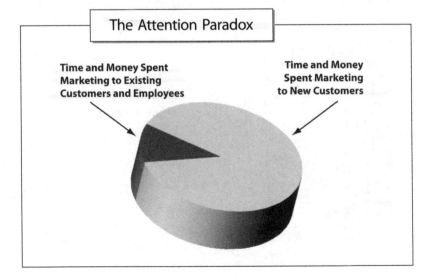

The Attention Paradox

Time and Money Spent Marketing to Existing Customers and Employees

Time and Money Spent Marketing to New Customers

and your employees as an army of individuals. This is not about having more people. By now, you know that faceless companies have people; real companies have individuals. The goal is to have a group of individuals who all believe the same thing, and have the right tools to tell that message to the rest of the world.

In order for this goal to be achieved, many new media industry experts say that you (as a business owner or key staff member in a large organization) need to give up control. These experts argue that this is the only way to interact in this age of consumer empowerment. And this leads me to my first counterintuitive piece of advice of the book.

The new power of consumers does not make the world wild, lawless, or untamable. The overprescribed advice to simply give up all control is a defeatist way of looking at what is happening. The smarter marketers know that the future is about participation and the conversa-

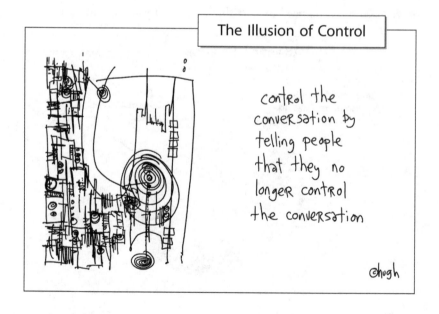

The Illusion of Control

control the conversation by telling people that they no longer control the conversation

@hugh

tion cannot be one-sided. *This means that you are not giving up control, but sharing it.* You need to have your own voice and it cannot simply be the same corporate voice you are used to using.

There are many situations in which you can have a conversation and yet maintain control in a nondomineering way. A moderated blog is a good example of this. Essentially, the point is to act like your consumers. Pete Blackshaw at Nielsen Online calls this the wave of *consumer emulation* and points to this as one of the top trends shaping the future of marketing. The main idea is that if you are going to participate you need to emulate your customers' behavior, borrowing methods that they use to communicate to shape your own communications. This does not mean pretending to be a 16-year-old girl and posting comments on blogs; I think we can all agree that's not going to work. It *does* mean having a real identity and relaying it in a way that mirrors how your customers are talking to one another.

Those readers familiar with word-of-mouth marketing (WOM) will recognize that this conversation is typically grounded in the core principles of how to do word-of-mouth marketing. A good example of how one company used word-of-mouth marketing to create an authentic identity is BzzAgent, one of the most conversational companies ever created.

Notes from the Central Hive

The first sign that BzzAgent is a company unlike any other comes with your very first call to the head office in Boston. As you are being transferred to the person you wish to speak with, you are put on hold and then suddenly thrust into an ongoing conversation, instead of the usual background music, as a participant in a conference call. Confused, your first thought is probably that you must have been transferred by mistake into a boardroom discussion. So you try to speak up, but no one answers.

Slowly, you realize that being thrown into this conversation is BzzAgent's not so subtle way of telling you that they do things differently. As Dave Balter, founder of BzzAgent, explains, "Most companies want to believe their personality can be shaped by revamping their logo or updating their Web site. But these are superficial adjustments; behavior is the foundation that creates personality."

At BzzAgent, behavior means everything from having a determined (some call it angry) bee for a logo to calling their head office the "central hive." Each element embodies a distinct choice. As Balter further describes, "While BzzAgent's brand stands for WOM, our personality is comprised of something incredibly different: innovation and transparency." So when the company received a large chunk of venture capital funding from investors in December 2005, they had the perfect recipe for losing the identity they had worked so hard to build—lots of cash and a coming influx of many employees in a short time frame. For Balter, there was only one way to grow and stay true to the core belief of BzzAgent, and that was by making sure all of his employees and customers were watching.

To do this, he sent an e-mail to John Butman, his friend and coauthor of *Grapevine*, hoping to launch an experiment in what he called "organizational transparency."

From: Dave Balter, BzzAgent, Inc.
To: John Butman
Subject: Project on My Mind, I Can't Shake
Date: Thu, 05 Jan 2006 23:10:37 -0500

Doc —
I got an idea.
What do you think about a 3 month on-staff writing gig at BzzAgent.

It's simple. The company just got about $15 million in funding [true].

I want to have you document the company for 3 months—in writing. To the world. We'll set it up as a blog—people can respond to the daily postings.

You hang out in the office. Write about the real internal workings. What's really happening.

It's like a reality show. But written. Cheap to produce. Fun to watch. We take the idea of the BeeLog and we turn it up a dozen notches. In real time. Do something no company has ever done before.

We could get very creative with this. Plus, I think you'd like the energy in the office right now–and would enjoy your energy around as well. [you can certainly work on other projects while there, if you want].

You in?

Dave

Butman agreed—and over the next 90 days, he dutifully chronicled the growth of the company. There were blog posts on everything from the excitement of moving to a new office location, to the personal stories of individual employees based in far-flung locations. Reading it, you understood what it was like to work at BzzAgent. It was real.

The blog has been up and running for over a year—and BzzAgent has continued to grow and make unique choices that fuel loyalty among their agents and make the brand something worth talking about. One element that may be most central to how BzzAgent differs from most organizations is how they use internal communication to create an exciting, productive workplace. Employees are encouraged to blog and share their thoughts not just with one another, but also with the outside world.

Seth Minkin, a longtime BzzAgent collaborator and recently appointed Artist-in-Residence is the unofficial voice of BzzAgent, through his many drawings and contributions to the culture of the Central Hive. Below is an example of one drawing he did as part of a project called The Bento Box designed to "balance corporate transparency with creative freedom," in which BzzAgent employees shared thoughts with each other about the state of the company and what it stood for. The drawing's theme was decided on collaboratively by the company's employees.

NO SHIFTY BZZ PRACTICES

Minkin is just one member of the team who has become an unofficial spokesperson for the brand. Another is BzzAgent Jono, who is the one member of the Central Hive that is on a first-name basis with most of the several hundred thousand "agents" now registered on the site. The reason is that Jono (pronounced "John-o") is the one who communicates updates to all of them, and sends the initial letter to them when they first join a campaign.

When any BzzAgent makes it to the home office or sees a video online, the most often expressed reaction is surprise. People don't expect Jono to be a real person. When they learn that he is, it is just another reason for them to believe that BzzAgent is the ultimate company that lives its personality through its actions, and the actions of every one of its employees.

To get there, they have learned how to take advantage of the single most important phenomenon to come out of the new social media era—the rise of the accidental spokesperson. To understand this evolution, Chapter 2 will start by looking at the incredible story of how one cartoon drawn on the back of a business card is helping reinvent the corporate culture at one of the largest technology companies in the world.

The Sellevator Pitch[2]

Being faceless doesn't work anymore. Today you need to have a company of *individuals* (instead of people) who are empowered to *share* control with your customers.

---

[2] Sell the idea of this chapter in the length of an elevator ride.

Chapter 2

The Accidental Spokesperson

How Unlikely Voices Are Shaping Your Brand

We live in a time when people don't trust big companies. Headlines gush with tales of malfeasance, abuse, and the old-fashioned plunder, but that's just part of the problem. There's a general perception that large companies are run by slick lawyers and book-fixing accountants who oversee armies of obedient dronelike employees. Companies are perceived as monoliths without souls. In short, we see no humanity.

—Opening to *Naked Conversations*

Microsoft used to be evil. At least in the eyes of most consumers, the company was seen as bent on world domination. Given the worldwide adoption and popularity of Microsoft's operating systems to run the majority of computers, the possibility of this domination seemed very real. Despite Steve Ballmer's frequent protestation that Microsoft was not a monopoly but just controlled market share, most people weren't buying it.

This fear that Microsoft would rule each of our lives through an operating system monopoly led to countless problems for the brand over the past decade, including a negative reputation with the public, hundreds of legal battles, and low employee morale. When Google first emerged, it defined its mission entirely as being the opposite of Microsoft, even using

Microsoft to inspire its now-famous guiding principle: Don't be evil. That was when Google was going to be the anti-Microsoft and save the world. Then Google bought YouTube, entered more aggressively into the advertising business, launched new mega initiatives like Android and Knol, and now seems to be heading along its own path to world domination.

Microsoft, on the other hand, doesn't seem as evil as it once did (its recent takeover bid for Yahoo! not withstanding). How did this happen? No one issued a company-wide memorandum asking employees to be a little less evil every day. Nonetheless, over a relatively short time, the negative image that had plagued one of the largest technology companies in the world, bringing lawsuits, poor public perception, and distrust for more than a decade had melted away. How did this happen if it was not through some policy change or a brilliant new marketing campaign? The phenomenon responsible for Microsoft's journey from evil to acceptable is related to the rise of the *accidental spokesperson*.

The book *Naked Conversations* by Robert Scoble and Shel Israel takes you inside this journey, beginning with a discussion of Microsoft's transformation in a chapter titled "Soul of the Borg." The chapter title is a geeky allusion to *Star Trek: The Next Generation,* linking what ultimately happened at Microsoft to the part human part machine drones from the popular sci-fi series. But the premise of the entire book is that blogs were the way that Microsoft found its identity and began to be perceived as something other than a faceless corporation with a secret James Bond villain–like plot for world domination.

Bloggers like Joshua Allen, Robert Scoble, and many others were profiled in the book as the real voices from within the walls of Redmond, Washington, portraying Microsoft as more than a "monolith without a soul." They were the first accidental spokespeople for the brand—not authorized or trained by their marketing or PR teams, but still communicating with customers in a direct and honest way that humanized the brand.

Yet despite the conclusion of *Naked Conversations*, this group of superstar bloggers alone did not reinvent Microsoft or the way the company began to see itself. Something more fundamental was changing at the company and it was a shift in the way that employees started to see themselves and their company. Microsoft was a place where people could do great things. These bloggers were accidental spokespeople for the brand and did volumes to humanize it, but the journey for Microsoft only started there.

In late 2006, Hugh MacLeod, illustrator and author of the popular Gaping Void blog, created a drawing on the back of a business card that he called the Blue Monster, and circulated it among his friends who worked at Microsoft. The cartoon was a caricature of a blue monster and issued a challenge to all Microsoft employees.

The Blue Monster

microsoft.com   stormhoek.com   gapingvoid.com   @hugh macleod 2006

MacLeod dubbed this activity "The Blue Monster Project" and described it as working on several levels:

> Microsoft telling its employees to change the world or go home.
> Microsoft employees telling their colleagues to change the world or
>   go home.
> Everybody else telling Microsoft to change the world or go home.
> And so forth.

Soon after he created the illustration, it went viral inside Microsoft. Employees began passing it from person to person. It appeared tacked onto cubicle walls. And though this started in the UK, where Hugh lives, the Blue Monster rapidly went global at Microsoft. As Hugh wrote nearly a year after the cartoon first appeared, "The Blue Monster is like a blog. It allows Microsoftees to express their humanity without going through commitees."[1]

The inspiration behind the illustration was a conversation Hugh had with a manager at Microsoft named Steve Taylor. Taylor put a Microsoft perspective on the power of the Blue Monster, describing what the drawing symbolized for "Microsoftees."

> For too long, Microsoft has allowed other people—the media, the competition and their detractors, especially—to tell their story on their behalf, instead of doing a better job of it themselves. We firmly believe that Microsoft must start articulating their story better— what they do, why they do it, and why it matters—if they're to remain happy and prosperous long-term.

The Blue Monster became an accidental spokesperson that reinvented the way that Microsoft employees had started to think about the purpose

---

[1] From a "Tweet" in Hugh's Twitter microblogging stream on 11/18/07. (Should this be called a "twuote"?)

of their company and their own role in it. It symbolized the kind of place where they wanted to work, and what Microsoft could be. This was a place where people wanted to believe they were changing the world, not just writing code or building tools. The drawing depicted the reason people joined Microsoft in the first place, and why they stayed.

It was also a way for outsiders to send a message to Microsoft. Blogger and self-described "accidental technologist" J.P. Rangaswami noted on his blog, "People *want* Microsoft to change. That is the essence of what made the Blue Monster such a hit, it was a way of people *outside* Microsoft telling people *in* Microsoft of the intense need for change."[2]

The message, it seems, is getting through. Today, the Blue Monster diagram hangs in Microsoft offices worldwide. It has spawned a Facebook group with thousands of members, a new custom wine label from Stormhoek available only to Microsoft employees, and, most important, it has reignited the passion that many Microsoft employees have for the power of their jobs and what is possible.

In late 2007, just over a year after the cartoon was first drawn, Hugh MacLeod himself noted in an interview with the *Financial Times:*

> We started an underground movement within Microsoft, and we knew one day the guys in suits would finally take notice. That moment has finally arrived.[3]

What Microsoft realized in several ways was that the true power of an accidental spokesperson (whether it is a blogger or a drawing) comes from him or her having natural authenticity. Every day more and more brands are starting to realize this as well. The majority, though, are still focused on controlling messages and preventing any possibility of these types

[2] http://confusedofcalcutta.com/2007/05/25/musing-about-outsides-and-insides/
[3] http://www.ft.com/cms/s/0/4fe8aad0-62de-11dc-b3ad-0000779fd2ac.html

of spokespeople expressing themselves. Blame for this falls mostly on the leaders of organizations who have been trained over time to avoid accidents.

The Art of Embracing Accidents

People don't tend to see accidents as a good thing. Usually when you hear about an accident, it is related to a car crash, or an inadvertent "Reply to all" e-mail embarrassingly sent to the wrong people, or some other event in your personal or professional life that you would rather forget. When you Google the word "accident," it returns sites like www.car-accidents.com and keyword ads for personal injury lawyers. Clearly, our opinion of accidents is not good. It's no surprise, then, that many marketing teams devote significant energy to finding ways to avoid accidents by keeping tight control of their messages and communications.

The problem with this approach is that sometimes accidents have a positive effect. The Post-it note was created by accident. So were Cornflakes, Teflon, the Slinky, and countless other product-related discoveries. Even one of the most successful marketing campaigns of the past decade featured a spokesperson located by accident—Jared from Subway.

Why People Believed Jared

Jared Fogle was never supposed to be a Subway spokesperson. He was just a guy in Indiana who used to weigh over 400 pounds and had been profiled in the local paper for losing more than 100 pounds in three months on his self-described "Subway diet." In spite of protests by the national brand manager at Subway as well as the typical legal resistance that accompanies most great marketing ideas, Subway's advertising agency decided to shoot the first ad with Jared for free to run as a regional spot only. It took off and has since become a national campaign and Jared became an advertising icon for Subway.

What was the allure of Jared? He was certainly not a celebrity, but he was *real*. The diet may not work for you, but it worked for Jared (as the first voice-overs on the ads proclaimed), and that was pretty compelling. He was a real person who had an authentic story and people believed it. The success of Jared is one example of how a brand can find and involve its enthusiasts in marketing, but using Jared was not completely an accident. He may have been discovered by chance, but he was deliberately cast in the role of spokesperson by an agency unafraid to take advantage of the good fortune of finding him.

As the Subway example shows, embracing accidents in marketing is the product of a mindset that can lead to great success. In Subway's case, the company found an official spokesperson through the story of a real brand enthusiast. However, instead of a company coming upon the perfect spokesperson by chance, the far more common situation is that brands specifically choose their deliberate spokespeople.

The Deliberate Spokesperson

GO TO GUIDE p.245

Spokespeople humanize brands in order to raise their profile and combat facelessness. The degree of success with which this happens, however, is variable. Isuzu owns the most classic example of a compelling brand salesperson ever created—"Joe Isuzu," a character that was portrayed as a slimy car salesman. The media and public loved Joe because he was funny. He was a great character played by a great actor. The only problem was that he portrayed a lying car salesman and did nothing to connect customers to the brand of Isuzu. It is very likely he even hurt the perception of the brand by the public, leading to their now well-known rapid decline in market share.

Joe Isuzu is just one example of a deliberate spokesperson, and he fits one particular type. As we will see, there are actually five key types of deliberate spokespeople that have been used for more than a century to try to humanize brands. Some have worked, and some haven't, but in order to truly understand the transformative power of the accidental spokesperson, we must first start by exploring the five types of deliberate spokespeople.

THE FIVE TYPES OF DELIBERATE SPOKESPEOPLE

Spokespeople	Why It Works (when it works)	Why It Fails (when it fails)
The Founder (Examples— James Dyson, David Ogilvy)	• Personal connection to brand • Real passion and knowledge	• Lacking charisma or speaking ability • Can be dismissed as biased
The Character (Examples— Singapore Girl, Tony the Tiger)	• Memorable and attention grabbing • Puts a face and identity to a brand	• Fabricated and not real • Often limited to catchphrases or taglines
The Authority (Examples—4 out of 5 dentists; infomercial authorities)	• Credible and unbiased third party • Believable due to subject expertise and perceived neutrality	• Can be limited to a product-focused message • Establishing credibility can be a challenge

Spokespeople	Why It Works (when it works)	Why It Fails (when it fails)
The Celebrity (Examples— Carmen Electra, Brad Pitt)	• Attention grabbing and high visibility • Quick way to generate awareness	• Questionable allegiance to brand • Perception that celeb is "paid to play"
The Enthusiast (Examples— Jared from Subway, Mikey)	• Demonstrate real, believable passion • Offers an authentic, credible opinion	• Lack of name recognition • Perception that enthusiast "sold out"

Spokesperson Type 1—The Founder

This is what every company starts with. In the beginning, there is always the founder or founders. They are behind the vision of the company and often may lend their names to the company as well. At an early stage in a company's evolution, the role of the spokesperson is usually taken by the founder(s).

Henry Ford (Ford Motor Company), Jamsetji Tata (Tata Group), and David Ogilvy (Ogilvy & Mather) were all the early spokespeople for their particular organizations. They are all also part of a different era in business. Today it has become equally common for founders to be displaced (voluntarily or not) by other types of spokespeople as a company evolves. Bill Gates (Microsoft), Phil Knight (Nike), Pierre Omidyar (eBay), and Andy Grove (Intel) are all examples of individuals who have taken a quieter role in the communications and marketing functions of their respective companies.

In other cases, no matter how much time has passed since a company was founded, the founder remains a consistent outward face for an organization. Craig Newmark, founder of Craigslist, is an example of this type of consistent founder-spokesperson. Tim Horton was another example (until his untimely death). He was one of Canada's most beloved hockey players, who founded a chain of coffee and doughnut shops that bear his name and now operate in nearly 3,000 locations across Canada and more than 350 in the United States.

As we will further discuss later in this chapter, James Dyson is one of the most successful examples of a founder working very effectively as a spokesperson. Wally Amos is another such example, building his Famous Amos cookie brand around his personal identity. In an interview with *The Wall Street Journal* in 2006, he talked about the importance of personality to building his brand.

> In this day and age when everything is so big, big is not better. Big is just bigger. People buy from other people. People do business with other people. If you have a product that lends itself to you being the spokesperson for it, you can be the person out front. You've got to have a personality.[4]

The reason it does work is because founders can bring passion and credibility to a marketing message. People respect individuals who have a vision and have realized it, and most founders fit this category. Not every founder has the charisma or ability to be a convincing spokesperson, but

---

[4] "Building a Brand Around a Personality" http://online.wsj.com/article/S70716LORBER.html.

those brands that are able to use their founders often come closest to delivering on the promise of their founder's vision.

Spokesperson Type 2—The Character

When a brand is at the stage of beginning to focus on developing a marketing plan, a second type of spokesperson often emerges: the character. Characters used for advertising have a long history going back to icons like Tony the Tiger for Kellogg's Frosted Flakes or the Michelin Man for Michelin tires. In the glory days of advertising, these iconic product characters were beloved spokespeople for their brands. If not completely humanizing, at least they brought their respective brands to life and gave people something to connect with. The Singapore Girl has been the icon for Singapore Airlines since 1972 and today still demonstrates the brand's focus on quality and service.

Two of the more popular modern examples of using characters as spokespeople both come from Geico—the insurance company that wins a disproportionate number of marketing and advertising accolades considering the industry it is in. The company's characters, the Geico Cavemen (who react to the tagline that applying for Geico insurance is so easy "a caveman could do it") and the Geico gecko (a lizard with a British accent) have little to do with the brand. They are simply memorable choices used to deliver a relatively dry message about auto insurance. But they have managed to make auto insurance more interesting and stick in people's minds. The Cavemen even had their own (predictably) short-lived TV show in late 2007.

As you may have noticed, many of the examples where characters are being used as spokespeople directly relate to advertising campaigns. The more iconic characters are the ones that become inherent to a brand

and inseparable in the consumer's mind. You could never buy a box of Frosted Flakes without an image of Tony the Tiger, or take a Singapore Airlines flight without the Singapore Girl. The less successful ones are those that are used for a time and then retired to give way to the next marketing idea, like Jeeves from AskJeeves.com (since rebranded to Ask.com).

Whether a character perseveres in marketing and becomes a household name or ends up abandoned, what almost all character spokespeople have in common is that they are not chosen for their credibility or authenticity, but for their memorability or "stickiness." If consumers remember the character, then the job of the advertising has been accomplished. Consumers may or may not believe a character as a spokesperson (or understand why it makes sense), but in advertising if you remember it, most of the time a brand believes that the spokesperson has done its job.

Spokesperson Type 3—The Celebrity

Celebrities are often the most popular type of spokespeople for brands to choose. When it comes to connecting with consumers, though, the main problem with using celebrities is that most brands do a poor job of choosing a celebrity who can get past the credibility barrier. This barrier is signified by one critical question that often goes unasked, despite that it's usually the first one your customers ask (whether they realize it or not): would the celebrity talking to me about this product or service ever actually use it? Think about this the next time you see a celebrity spokesperson promoting a brand, and you may be amazed at the number of times the answer has to be no. One noteworthy example occurred back in 2000, with then-emerging British celebrity chef Jamie Oliver. He had a celebrity-spokesperson arrangement with Sainsbury (a UK-based retail grocery chain) and admitted on national television that he considered supermarkets like Sainsbury to be "factories" and preferred to get his ingredients from local organic markets. Another example was Ritz Camera's choice of Carmen Electra as model-spokesperson and creator of a series of aerobic striptease videos. The world of celebrity sponsorship is filled with lofty choices like these.

The reason most of these choices are made in the first place is that selecting a celebrity spokesperson has become an emotional process instead of a logical one. In many cases, brands fall in love with the idea of a certain celebrity and convince themselves to cast a celebrity whose effectiveness is questionable (and who is typically expensive) into the role of spokesperson. The main reason that many celebrity-spokesperson campaigns don't work is there is no rational connection between the celebrity and the brand or product. When no one believes the celebrity talking about your product or service would ever actually be seen anywhere near it, you have a problem.

Unfortunately, celebrity-spokesperson campaigns are the one place where I have most often seen intelligent and reasonable marketers approve irrational strategies. Supermodels are used to promote diet programs, famous singers for laptops, athletes for products they secretly don't use. The list of bad spokesperson choices goes on and on. There is, however, one interesting exception: celebrity spokespeople tend to have a great impact in social-marketing.

When celebrities work on marketing campaigns for social causes, it is usually because they have some personal connection to the issue and belief in the organization they are helping (or because of a court-mandated order, but let's pretend those situations are rare and unusual). In many cases, this belief means a celebrity is willing to work for little or no money. This combination can create a highly effective campaign in which the celebrities turn out to be the ideal spokespeople. For example, let's look at the ONE campaign to alleviate global poverty that has made and continues to make history.

A large factor in the success of this campaign was the volume of star power it managed to bring together, including the voices of many global celebrities such as Bono, Brad Pitt, George Clooney, Salma Hayek, and Djimon Hounsou. The campaign offers the inspiring message that we all have the power to reduce global poverty by uniting. When used appropriately, celebrities can harness their fame to support a singular cause as they did in the case of ONE. When used inappropriately, they become nothing more than expensive mouthpieces reading messages from a cue card that everyone knows they are being paid to read.

Spokesperson Type 4—The Authority

The authority is the one type of spokesperson who more than any other can cross over and behave like other types of deliberate spokespeople. For example, a founder or celebrity can also be an authority. An authority is a subject matter expert who offers a credible opinion because of his or her familiarity with the product category or industry. This type of spokesperson usually offers an endorsement of a product or service as their main message. While sometimes founders or celebrities can also be positioned as authorities, an authority does not need to have fame or an existing affiliation with a company to be effective.

A medium where you will commonly find this type of spokesperson is infomercial programming on television. Those inexpensively produced television segments are designed to offer you a detailed look into how a product can and should be used, presented by an individual who you believe to be an authority either because he is a user of the product or she works in an industry or role that qualifies him or her as an authority in some believable way. Hair loss treatments are sold by men who are now slightly less bald than they once were. Exercise machines are demonstrated by personal trainers. Cleaning products are tested and vouched for by moms of particularly slovenly teenagers. When four out of five dentists agree on the clear superiority of a particular type of toothpaste, no one is supposed to pay any attention to that fifth dentist.

The best authorities are the ones who consumers can believe would authentically use a product and are genuinely passionate about it. The only inconsistency in the consumer's mind that may be difficult to resolve is the knowledge that despite the authority figure loving and endorsing the product, he or she is still getting paid to do it.

Spokesperson Type 5—The Enthusiast

The enthusiast is the last category of deliberate spokesperson, and one that has typically been the most difficult for brands to locate and use. The famous "Mikey" from the legendary TV Quaker Oats Life cereal TV ads from the late 1970s and early '80s was one type of solution to this problem: a finicky fabricated four-year-old who hated everything, except his Life cereal. The call from his brothers in the ad spawned more than a decade of people saying to each other at random, "Mikey likes it!" Still, the character Mikey was made up, and though it worked at the time, to try to use a similar tactic today would likely not succeed as well. In the social media era, these sorts of imagined situations can no longer carry as much weight as a real story with real people.

As the example of Subway's Jared proves, using a *real* enthusiast as a spokesperson is a much better strategy. However, the problem with using enthusiasts like Jared is that they can be difficult to locate and very often are only discovered by accident. It is hardly a reliable way to find a spokesperson and certainly not as easy as calling the publicist for a celebrity and negotiating the rates to do a half day of media interviews from a studio somewhere.

Luckily, finding these enthusiasts is not as difficult a task as it once was. Today, brand enthusiasts are all around, and they are vocal about their enthusiasm. Through review sites, forums, blogs, word of mouth, and online searches, brands can more easily find their enthusiasts than ever before. The challenge is no longer finding enthusiasts; the present reality is that an entirely new breed of spokespeople is emerging that does not fit into one of the five types outlined so far. These new spokespeople are sometimes passionate brand enthusiasts (but there are sometimes equally passionate brand detractors). They can come from within your organization or have no affiliation at all. The only thing that unites them is that they are speaking for your brand, and they are not "authorized" to do it. These are your *accidental* spokespeople.

The Uncontrollable Rise of the Accidental Spokesperson

Accidental spokespeople are not relaying official marketing messages. They can be loyal customers, dedicated partners, or vocal employees. The thing that unites them is that their openness and thoughts are linked closely to the brand they talk about. Hacking Netflix, Starbucks Gossip, and The Unofficial Apple Weblog (TUAW) are all blogs that have become accidental spokespeople for the brands that they write about. They are not controlled by the brands they describe, but they influence perception about those brands in a powerful way.

Accidental spokespeople are not just bloggers, either. People who are contributing to Wikipedia about your brand, active members of message boards and online communities, passionate customers who recommend purchases to friends on social networks, and every one of your employees are all in a position to be accidental spokespeople for your brand. They are all around your brand at every level. Just how much do these types of accidental spokespeople matter?

To answer this question, let's look at the increasing popularity of Wikipedia. Most of us know Wikipedia as the world's largest and most complete encyclopedia of information. Every week there are new reports comparing the accuracy of Wikipedia with that of more established encyclopedias—and it usually comes out on top. Yet contrary to what most people may be tempted to believe, Wikipedia is not an encyclopedia of facts. It is an encyclopedia of perception. On a site where anyone can contribute any piece of content, the view that most often surfaces as the "truth" in an entry is the one that is perceived as the truth by the group.

No one knows this better than Jared Lanion—a technologist who sees himself as the originator of the term *virtual reality*. In 2006, he wrote an often quoted essay called "Digital Maoism: The Hazards of the New Online Collectivism."[5] His article was in part based on his own personal experience of having tried to edit his own Wikipedia entry to remove the description "filmmaker" from it since he did not believe his one attempt at a short film qualified him for this title. Each time he changed it, the "Wikipedia goblins" (as he called them) changed it back. As Lanion realized, and lamented in his essay, the encyclopedia of perception can sometimes be more powerful than the truth.

Blogging can have a similar story effect, which means that your accidental spokespeople are the ones that can shape what the world sees as the truth about your brand. This is not to say that the way to deal with this is simply to sit back and let it happen. I mentioned earlier that giving up control is not the answer.

Sharing control means finding a way to have your deliberate spokespeople coexist with your accidental ones. To help you to learn how to do

[5] http://www.edge.org/3rd_culture/lanier06/lanier06_index.html.

this, the rest of this chapter will take you through three examples of brands that have managed to accomplish it through blogs—which can be one of the best ways to use your accidental spokespeople.

The first example is of a brand that chose to embrace its most vocal customer and make his the voice of the brand. The second is a story of a brand that allowed an executive to start a blog, with stunningly positive results. The last is a story of one of the world's largest and most paranoid brands finally finding its voice through social media and its many accidental spokespeople.

Getting in Touch with Your Literary Side

Moleskine notebooks are not made of mole skin. They do, however, have a unique elastic band that keeps the notebook closed, and a distinctive sleek black cover that makes them easily recognizable. Inside each of the books is a romantic description of its history.

> The legendary notebook used by European artists and thinkers for the past two centuries from Van Gogh to Picasso, from Ernest Hemingway to Bruce Chatwin. This trusty, pocket-size travel companion held sketches, notes, stories and ideas before they were turned into famous images or pages of beloved books.

In a world where many people have abandoned writing in longhand, Moleskine celebrates the seemingly antiquated tradition of putting pen to paper, and doesn't apologize for it. A Moleskine notebook is meant to inspire your creative ability.

In the process of compiling and writing this book, I used several of them to collect my ideas. Like most Moleskine users, I have told many others about these iconic notebooks that make me feel just a bit more literary or artistic than perhaps I actually am. This is the real power of the books—they are aspirational. When you have one, you feel the latent desire to do something great with it.

No one knows this better than one of Moleskine's most passionate customers, Armand Frasco, who helped bring the Moleskine brand to life when he started a blog in 2004 called Moleskinerie, dedicated to all the things you could do with Moleskine notebooks. Within two years, he had become the unofficial voice of the Moleskine brand through his blog. In fact, his blog was so influential that when one distribution company was negotiating with another to purchase the rights for the United States, he was contacted and consulted for his opinion.

After that, he was extended an offer to become an official spokesperson of sorts and continue to run his blog with funding from Moleskine. As he described it, having his blog acquired offered him a venue in which to share his passion for the Moleskine notebooks and become an even more believable voice for the brand. In Armand's words:

> When you tell people who you are and what you believe in, they accept you. I never expected to become a voice for the brand, but blogs like this should end up integrated with the company. Because people know there is a real person behind it, they trust my voice.

Interestingly, since associating himself with Moleskine, Armand has also started a second blog about notebooks beyond just Moleskines called Notebookism. He describes the purpose of the second blog as allowing him to talk more broadly about his love of notebooks and all the things people can do with them. Ironically, this second effort might be lending even more credibility to his first. Each time he hosts a conversation online about anything relating to notebooks, he becomes more of an authority on the topic. People who are fans of one blog will likely become fans of the other. His underlying message is that people who know notebooks (like him) choose Moleskine.

The real story of how Moleskine has connected with Armand Frasco (his blog was officially acquired by Moleskine.com in January 2008) and Moleskinerie is a perfect example of how to embrace an accidental spokesperson. Armand is the ultimate citizen marketer,[6] and the type of accidental spokesperson that most brands dream of: one who is an authority on a topic, a vocal enthusiast about the brand, and willing to tell everyone he knows (and anyone else who will listen) just how much he loves their product. He started as a customer, became an accidental spokesperson, and then became a deliberate spokesperson for a brand willing to embrace him.

Of course, Armand was the type of customer that any business would be lucky to find. As the Microsoft example from early in this chapter showed, sometimes these passionate individuals can more readily come not from your customers, but from your employees.

Employees as Accidental Spokespeople

GO TO GUIDE *p.*248 I am an accidental spokesperson for the marketing and PR agency I work for. As a result of my marketing blog, what I write about reflects on my employer and though I try to be clear that I am not the official spokesperson for my company, the thoughts I share still reflect on the brand of the company I work for. My case is only one among hundreds of thousands of individuals who are rapidly taking on this new role without having expected to. They can come from any level of an organization. Sometimes this means an unexpected executive who becomes the trusted voice for a brand, and in other cases it is

---

[6] A term popularized by Jackie Huba and Ben McConnell's brilliant book by the same title, which also features Armand's story.

someone from far lower down in an organization. As we learned in Chapter 1, these unexpected voices were once the ones that companies used to work very hard to silence. Many companies are still fighting this battle.

Yet today more than ever these employees are breaking out and humanizing their companies in a noticeable way. They are writing passionately about subjects that relate to their jobs, building a following and becoming visible as influential voices. Most companies have great difficulty embracing these spokespeople. Bosses may feel threatened and long-standing policies may be challenged. It requires a shift in thinking to welcome these new spokespeople as voices from within and encourage them to continue to have a voice.

GO TO GUIDE p. 254

There are some companies that don't make this leap. These are the ones who fire employees for blogging about their business, place restrictive barriers against employees having voices, and forbid anyone from blogging about anything related to their business. Perhaps you work for a company like this, and if you do, you are likely reading this chapter and thinking that your brand is very far away from realizing the power of its employees' voices. If so, Chapter 5 will offer you some answers on how to help propel your company forward and get past some of the barriers you may be facing.

One of the most effective ways (which we will also discuss further in a related guide from Part Two) is to use a senior member of your team to break down these barriers and demonstrate to an organization the potential benefits of blogging. For an example of this, we can turn to one of the most effective corporate blogs being written today, and one that has done what few other companies have managed to do—build a blog that is a true voice of a company rather than one of a forthcoming and engaging individual. The blog is called Randy's Journal, and has been authored in turn by two different vice presidents of marketing, both sharing the same first name: Randy.

The Voices of Randy, in Two Acts

GO TO GUIDE p.250 When Randy Baseler decided to retire, Boeing didn't just stand to lose a popular and long-serving chief marketing officer. Over the course of several years, Randy had become the voice of Boeing to the world through Randy's Journal, one of the most respected corporate blogs in the world. Through his posts about the aviation industry, Boeing's ongoing battle with Airbus, and his experiences traveling around the world, his was among the rare corporate blogs that were fun to read even if you did not work in the industry within which it was written.

When you first start reading Randy's blog, the most obvious thing you notice is that it is not written in a corporate voice. While this may seem unexpected from a company like Boeing, it is certainly not unexpected in a blog. But Randy's Journal has a more authentic voice than most, because of the little things. When Randy was traveling on the road, his posts reflected that. He put a personal voice on everything, including announcements or corporate news that seemed tailor-made for a press release that would be ignored by everyone but a few loyal journalists.

When Randy was too busy traveling, he didn't post, and as a result, he became a voice that people trusted because quality mattered and he was upfront about his time constraints. To understand the real power of having a communications voice like this, it is easiest to look at the impact it can have in a moment of competition or crisis. One of the most telling examples came in early 2006 at a time when Airbus was running what Boeing felt were misleading ads and touting to the media the data point that the A320 cabin was "7 inches wider than the 737."

In an inspired post, Randy laid out his point of view not as a VP at Boeing, but as an aviation pro and frequent traveler who had actually flown on both planes.

Width is which?

The statement I seem to keep hearing and reading is that the A320 cabin is "7 inches wider than the 737." And that this somehow makes the Airbus product a more comfortable, more preferred airplane.

Well, okay, the A320 is about 7 inches (18 cm) wider. But the interesting thing about that assertion is that the "7-inch" difference is actually not a cabin measurement, but is measured from the exterior fuselage of the airplane.

Now, I'm not sure how many passengers choose to sit on the outside of an airplane, but I would think it's kind of breezy out there!

So let's talk about the inside, where you and I ride. Inside the cabin is what really matters, and that's where you'll realize there's little comfort difference between the Next-Generation 737s and the A320 family.

And at head and shoulder level—or seated eye height, as it's sometimes described—there's only a 2.8 inch (7.1 cm) difference between the two airplanes.

Once you realize that, you see that this amounts to less than a half inch more space per passenger. Or about the width of a pencil!

And when talking about these two airplane families, you might also want to consider something else. For short flights, passenger survey results tell us that the major influence on whether you think you had a good flight experience is on-time performance. And the Next-Generation 737 is the industry leader in technical reliability. In comparison, the A320 series has 40% more technical delays.

Later, Randy published a follow up to his earlier post.

14 March 2006

War of Inches

Airplane interiors—now that's a topic that really gets people squirming in their seats!

The blog we did a couple of weeks back about the so-called "7-inch" difference between the A320 and the 737 turned out to be one of the more controversial topics we've done.

Some people took it quite personally. We've now posted your thoughts on the subject in our comments section. For example:

"I am convinced that Boeing senior management does not fly their competitor's product in coach class."

Au contraire. As it happens, I just rode back-to-back flights on the 737 and A320 during my recent trip to Australia. I flew on Virgin Blue, on a Next-Generation 737. And I also flew on a Jetstar A320. They were both in an all-economy six abreast seating configuration. And quite frankly there was not much difference.

But I'm not trying to convince anybody one way or another, or trying to say that the 737 is better from a comfort point of view. I'm just saying that the difference is not great. And that on short-range flights, most people are more concerned about their fare and schedule.

This was not your standard corporate response. This was the real experience of an admittedly biased individual who nonetheless had actually sat in both planes and was telling customers exactly why his company's product was better than the competition, and doing it with a voice that you could believe. He even admitted that he does, in fact, fly economy class. Yes, losing a voice like Randy's to retirement was not going to be easy.

The issue was further complicated by the fact that Randy's blog had his name in it—and would therefore be hard to shift to someone else. As Boeing's communications specialist (and blog facilitator) Jim Condelles describes it, Boeing knew they would be keeping Randy's Journal as a Boeing blog but had anticipated changing the name. When new VP of Marketing Randy Tinseth was appointed, it became a natural transition to move from one Randy to another.

Randy Tinseth took over where the first Randy left off and the blog continues to offer a strong voice for the company. It was the first ever corporate blog spin-off (to use a TV term), but also demonstrated what Boeing understood about the power of having a key team member blogging. The first Randy always intended to offer insight and a voice for Boeing with the blog. What was surprising was just how much it became *the* voice. As Jim notes, "The growth and respect that [the blog] has developed are as remarkable as they have been unexpected." He describes the blog as a key asset in creating a dialogue with employees, investors, customers, aviation enthusiasts, and the media—and one of the first things that many people would ask about at Boeing enthusiast and media events.

The second Randy took on the charge of continuing that dialogue without losing a step. He didn't have to wait long for his first challenge. Just a few months after starting, on October 10, 2007, Boeing announced that the Dreamliner (its long-awaited flagship aircraft under development) would ship six months late. Randy's Journal was the first place many people turned and on it the new Randy offered a voice of admission (yes, it was late) along with the message of hope (it would still be great and game changing).

Soon after, when Boeing's greatest rival had its moment of glory by finally delivering the first of its own flagship aircraft—the colossal 525-seater A380, Randy offered a simple comment through a blog post:

> . . . there's no doubt that a tip of the hat is in order to Airbus on this milestone. We also salute Singapore Airlines, a great customer of ours and a leader in commercial aviation. Congratulations on a big delivery.

The message he intended to send was obvious: Boeing was going to be a first-class corporate citizen all the way. As the tale of two Randys shows, blogs can offer a way of giving your spokespeople real and authentic voices with which to communicate with customers. In Boeing's case, the choice to start a blog may have been made deliberately, but as Jim puts it, "no one at Boeing had any inkling that it would be so successful, or that it would be approaching one million individual visits at the end of its first three years. The blog was intended to be a small niche, spread by word of mouth only." This demonstrates an important point about the accidental spokesperson—that sometimes it is the popularity that is accidental, as one can rise from an unexpected (yet deliberate) source.

The next example is one from a company similar in size to Boeing that also slowly embraced social media with a few active individuals and is now finding ways to use those lessons to connect with its many fans across all areas of the technology industry.

Only the Paranoid Survive (or Blog)

Josh Bancroft is an open source guy. His describes his official title as "Social Technology Geek and Software Storyteller," and he writes a blog called Tiny Screenfuls. He lives his life in the open, shares his latest thoughts through streaming tools like Twitter, Flickr, and just about any other Web 2.0 site ending in "r" (with or without a vowel before the "r") that you can name. In late August 2006, he liveblogged the birth of his second child—sharing updates online from the hospital with his large community of online friends. The most interesting thing about Josh, though, is that he does all of this publicly while working at one of the largest companies in the world whose unofficial motto has become "Only the paranoid survive." His company is Intel and Josh is just one of a host of individuals who are picturing and driving a more conversational future for Intel despite its overwhelming size and internal complexity. The way that Josh and many others like him have managed to take a company whose culture has hinged for years on remaining paranoid and cultivate an open, engaging personality is a lesson in how small waves can make an impact in a big ocean.

By any estimate, Intel's ocean is larger than most. The company has more than 90,000 employees worldwide, ships the overwhelming majority of the world's microprocessors, and has relationships with just about every major computer manufacturer there is. The company's marketing is also legendary for how they have pioneered the approach on how to be a *component brand*—a concept they invented to describe a company that makes a product that is not sold alone, but made to go into another product. Every year the company provides millions of dollars in marketing support to their partners, part of which pays for the Intel image at the end of so many technology ads with the recognizable Intel four-note theme.

Still for all their brilliant integrated marketing, just a few short years ago, Intel had no blogs, no social media policies, a relatively secretive research process, and was a visibly closed company. In the past few years, the brand has shed its closed outlook and launched group blogs and open source communities, sponsored forums, and more. At a recent Consumer Electronics Show (CES) in Las Vegas, they had a team of dozens of people blogging, recording video, capturing questions in real time, and sharing voices of many Intel people with the world during the event. I was part of that team.

Today, there are many voices coming out of Intel that are all sharing a different experience of how the company is evolving, building new technology and products, and enabling the world to move ahead. There are dozens of accidental spokespeople for Intel, including Jeff Moriarty, Bryan Rhoads, Ken Kaplan, and many others across the world. Josh now describes himself and his role very differently, noting, "I used to be kind of lonely as the only 'Intel blogger,' but now, I'm in very rich and plentiful company."

The company now has group blogs from Brazil, Latin America, China, and Russia and has launched several open communities to more directly connect their employees to customers. Intel has found a way to embrace their internal accidental spokespeople, and found many voices worldwide to help humanize the brand. Between the writing and the publishing of this book that number will likely have tripled.

Accidentally Deliberate?

So far we have seen several examples in this chapter of what I have called accidental spokespeople coming from within an organization, including

Jono at BzzAgent, Randy (and the other Randy) at Boeing, and lots of individuals within Intel. I also shared one example of a customer becoming an accidental spokesperson (Armand's story with Moleskine), and will share several others later in the book.

The one potential contradiction that you may see in all this is that many of these accidental spokespeople don't seem very "accidental" at all. In fact, some may seem pretty well orchestrated and decidedly deliberate. For example, how can I call the second Randy an accidental spokesperson when he was clearly authorized by Boeing to blog before he started? Also, all of the examples of accidental spokespeople are now in positions where there are very *deliberate* spokespeople. So the question you may be asking now is why have we spent so much time talking about accidental spokespeople when every one is a deliberate choice?

The answer is twofold. First, to help you identify the people who are speaking for your brand, whether they are simply out there and not connected to your brand, or they are voices that you know about, but that are drawing a surprising amount of attention and being seen as a spokesperson rather than simply another voice from your company. The second goal is an idea we first discussed early in the chapter—embracing accidents. Your ultimate goal should be never to have any accidental spokespeople, because as soon as you identify them, you need to be thinking about ways to embrace them.

This is not about ownership. Some of your most powerful voices of support may come from outside of your organization and you should be willing to keep it that way. Embracing them means giving them the content, attention, and access they need to tell a compelling story. Having spokespeople for your brand who are not part of your official communications channel is a good thing, as long as you can find a way to embrace rather than ignore them.

The Dark Side of Accidental Spokespeople

So far we have focused on the positive opportunities that accidental spokespeople offer for marketing and communications, whether they happen to be a top executive, an employee, or a customer. It is important to also talk about the potential for a dark side, which comes from a group of people that a *New York Times* article in late 2004 first termed the "determined detractors."[7] These are the people who are passionate about how much they dislike your brand, and want to do everything they can to make sure others know about it.

I briefly spoke about these individuals in the opening of Chapter 1, but it is important to note that they have an equally strong opportunity to become your accidental spokespeople, in a negative way. There are many ways to deal with individuals like this, many of which we will cover in Chapter 5, which is dedicated to strategies for overcoming detractors, roadblocks, and other dangers. We will also discuss ways of dealing with these detractors and changing their perceptions or countering their arguments.

Getting Past the "Who?"

This chapter has been all about answering the question: who? Who is talking about your brand? Who is influential? Who are your spokespersons? We know why faceless companies don't work anymore and how the rise of the accidental spokesperson is changing who communicates and shapes perceptions of brands. Now we need to turn to the broader idea of personality and how to define it for your organization.

According to the usual way that a marketing strategy is developed, the approach we have taken so far in this book might seem odd. For exam-

---

[7] "Marketing's Flip Side: The 'Determined Detractor,'" http://www.nytimes.com/2004/12/27/business/media/27adco.html.

ple, we have spent so much time talking about the spokespeople for a message before delving more deeply into *what the message is*. The reason for this is simple: the spokespeople for your brand are already out there talking about you. As a result, they are not messengers for the strategic messages you will create as much as they are influential channels that already have an audience which you need to consider.

After you start to see them in this way, you will understand why it is necessary to know who they are before you can craft a strategy on how to best connect with them. In addition, paying attention to what they say offers clues to how you might define the personality of your brand. In the next chapter, you will learn a new model for defining your organization's personality and a way of demonstrating it to all of your spokespeople.

The Sellevator Pitch

Your accidental spokespeople are the employees or customers who are speaking for your brand already (often without your approval or knowledge) and your first challenge is to find ways to embrace these individuals.

Chapter 3

A Signature Is Not Enough

How to Define Your Organization's Personality

In 1872, a traveling salesman changed the landscape of American retail. Before him, the only way rural farmers could purchase goods was through middlemen like him, who created a monopoly, allowing them to over-charge for everything. The salesman's name was Aaron Montgomery Ward and when he published the first mail-order catalog the world had ever seen, he started a brand-new industry. His catalog, more than 50 years later, was exhibited by the Grolier Club (a society of bibliophiles in New York City) as one of the 100 books that have had the greatest influence on the life and culture of the American people.

Yet Ward's creation had an unintended side effect: he killed the sig-nature. His mail-order catalog was also the commonly recognized start of direct mail as a marketing tactic. Before then, signatures were important. Important communications were affixed with a wax seal for a signature. Documents creating governments and laws were put into effect with flow-ing signatures. A signature used to mean something.

Fast-forward to today and think about all the direct mail you recently received in your mailbox. Every one of those letters has a fake signature on it, promising you that you are a sweepstakes winner or offering you the preapproved credit card that can solve all of your financial woes. The signature on each is an obvious piece of "photoshoppery" meant to put a human name upon the worst of form letters. Signatures have lost their significance because of the prevalence of communications like this. Perhaps it is wrong to blame it all on Ward. In truth, it was the marketing industry that killed the signature.

Here are three reasons why signatures don't work anymore.

1. They can be easily forged.
2. They carry little weight without context.
3. They are no longer unique or personal.

And if signatures have lost their impact, where does that leave brands that try to focus solely on finding a signature element in their product or service to talk about? To try to answer this question, let's look at one of the largest automotive repair franchises in the United States, which built its business on two principles: its signature service and the importance of convenience.

Convenience Is No Longer King

Jiffy Lube was founded in 1979 in response to the decline of full-service gas stations during the 1970s. Often called the "McDonald's of the auto service industry," both out of scorn and admiration by its competitors, Jiffy Lube pioneered the quick oil change business with its focus on speed and consistent service above all else.

The problem for Jiffy Lube is that convenience is not as important as it once was. In a prescient book published in 2000 called *The Soul of the New Consumer*, authors David Lewis and Darren Bridger chronicled the shift away from convenience by introducing the idea that authentic-

ity and convenience were at two opposing ends of a pole (or spectrum).
Today's consumers, they argued, were more involved, more informed, and
more likely to value authenticity above convenience. Convenience alone
was no longer enough. Jiffy Lube offers real proof of this point, as their
focus on convenience and speed has caused the company some problems
in the past decade.

Consumers may get the same checklist of items completed by their
signature service as they always did, but a quick search on the brand will
lead to hundreds of stories of negative customer experiences. Ask any
independent mechanic about Jiffy Lube and many will readily have a story
to tell about a time when they had to address a problem in a customer's
car that they believe was related to a service that a customer had done at
Jiffy Lube. Of course, none of this represents a truth about Jiffy Lube
(and they are likely no worse than any other automotive maintenance
provider), however it does create a wealth of negative word of mouth.
Among the online reviews you can find about Jiffy Lube, there are very
few glowing reports, and an increasing number of fan sites dedicated to
negative experiences with the brand have appeared. In a telling warning
sign, a higher and higher percentage of the online word of mouth on
Jiffy Lube is not so good.

This is not to single out this one brand. The problem facing Jiffy
Lube is the same one facing many other companies in the world today.
It falsely believes it has found a way to stand out and expends all its
effort and communications budget talking about its signature service and
convenience—both attributes that no longer set the company apart.
Instead, it should be finding a way to address the one emotion that any
customer who has ever had to visit a new automotive service shop will
relate to: vulnerability.

Marketing to Vulnerable Customers

Whenever they drive into an auto repair shop, people are vulnerable to being taken for a ride (figuratively speaking, that is) and to being placed in a situation where they have no option but to agree to whatever the mechanic suggests. After all, who is really going to shop around for competitive offers when you are already at one auto repair shop? Even if you were willing, your car may not be drivable. It is the ultimate sales hostage situation: where you are unable to avoid being taken advantage of and must give your trust reluctantly to someone who may or may not be trustworthy.

Many people believe that mechanics know this and are therefore mentally expecting to be unfairly treated. It is not a pleasant experience. What people really want is to be able to trust their mechanic. But trust usually takes time, so how can you earn it in what is meant to be a quick experience?

Oil Can Henry's, a regional franchise with branches in only seven states, may have the answer. As a much smaller and less recognized regional chain of automotive services centers, it has several unique service features that are all centered on fostering more trust between customers and staff. In addition to its own "Famous 20 Point" oil change service (an element that directly, and effectively, challenges Jiffy Lube), the focus at Oil Can Henry's is on building a relationship. Their tagline reads "The One You Can Trust" and every interaction with the company is meant to follow through on this promise.

The key insight that allows Oil Can Henry's to do this is the insight that if its customers are able to watch a mechanic work on their car, it automatically creates a feeling of ease and encourages trust. Of course, in most auto repair shops standing above the mechanic watching his every move would be awkward or impossible. Instead, you are shown to a waiting room with crusty old issues of *Sports Illustrated,* a TV tuned to soap operas or local news, stale coffee, and the distinct aroma of spilled oil.

At Oil Can Henry's, there are no waiting rooms. You stay in your and watch the mechanic work on custom TV screens that show a live video feed from underneath your car. Being able to stay in your car is nice, as is their commitment to explain what is happening with your car. They will even bring you coffee and the paper to read in your car while you wait.

What Oil Can Henry's knows about personality is that it is more than having one or two signature service things that you can do for everyone. It is about offering a unique experience that fulfills a need and gets customers to talk about it to others as a result.

As I first stated earlier in the book, a personality has three core qualities—it is unique, authentic, and talkable. A signature service may be unique for a short time, but eventually others will offer the same service and it will no longer be enough to make the company stand out. The great brands are the ones that can be more than just unique.

The rest of this chapter will help you to learn how to develop all three qualities. To help get you started, I will introduce a new way of thinking about personality. To introduce this approach, let's start by looking at the methods used by what is arguably the most personality-driven group of companies and brand in the world: Virgin.

Virgin Gets Mile High in America

When the Virgin brand is mentioned, the first image that likely comes into your head is that of Sir Richard Branson, the self-described "adventure capitalist," who has often been called "the world's greatest entrepreneur." He's been called lots of other things too, but regardless of whether you like him or not, his approach to launching new businesses is unarguably successful. When Virgin enters a new industry, you can assume it will challenge the long-held assumptions of that industry. This is an effect I have seen over and over with the brand through firsthand experience.

I have had the pleasure, so far, of working on two different launches of new Virgin companies in my career: first on the launch of the Virgin Money Credit Card in Australia in 2003, and more recently on the launch of the long-awaited Virgin America, a domestic airline for the United States.

When I helped launch the Virgin Money Credit Card, our entire campaign was based on giving your old card the "plastic surgery" it needed. The credit card itself had one rounded corner, giving the physical card a unique look that set it apart from others. Virgin Mobile also offered customers the ability to pay as you go without signing lengthy contracts and even poked fun at how competitors charged extra for essential services with billboards that proclaimed "Voicemail is like sex. . .you shouldn't have to pay for it."

The Virgin Group has launched a long list of new businesses that demonstrate the individuality of the Virgin brand, including:

- Virgin Brides—they sell wedding dresses (obviously; shame on you if you thought otherwise!).
- Virgin Galactic—on a quest to be the first commercial spacecraft-carrier in 2009.
- Virgin LimoBike—a deluxe limo service in the UK—on a motorcycle.
- Virgin Experience Days—a collection of unique life experiences that can be given as gifts.

When it comes to the businesses Virgin is best known for, outside of its music business, these are most certainly within the travel industry. Travel is a particular passion for Richard Branson himself and the brand is increasing its reach in the industry with both international and domestic airlines, including Virgin Atlantic (for transatlantic flights), Virgin Blue (in Australia), Virgin Nigeria (in Africa), and in 2007 the long-debated launch of Virgin America.

The reason for the debate was that the American domestic airline market is notoriously one of the toughest for a new entrant. Customer satisfaction scores are at an all-time low. Terror alerts and inconveniences caused by fears of terrorism are omnipresent. In late 2007 when Virgin America finally got its wings through U.S. government approval allowing it to start flying domestically, many experts expressed concern and wonder that Branson would even go into such a market.

Virgin America started right away by changing the way that the business of U.S. domestic air travel was conducted, and, more important, experienced by passengers. First, during the time it was still waiting to get its flights in air, Virgin partnered with what many consider the most popular blog in the world, Boing Boing, to run a contest to name one of their planes. The resulting name, *Unicorn Chaser,* built enormous buzz through the blog's huge audience, a tactic that was also used for the launch of Virgin Atlantic a few years earlier. Both airlines were a throwback to an era where flying was elite, prestigious, and executed with much more fanfare. As a launch stunt, the names of the planes gave a personality to each flight.

In addition to participation in naming, passengers on Virgin America flights were treated to brand-new custom-designed planes that included lots of long-awaited features, including a seatback entertainment system with on-demand movies, a plug for a laptop in every seat, the ability to order food directly from the seatback, and what is perhaps the single most viral feature on their flights, a feature that many people love, seat-to-seat chat. Although not for everyone, this technology allows you to start instant messaging conversations with any other passenger on the plane who has opened his or her profile to be contacted (of course, there is an invisibility option as well for privacy). Perhaps most significant, the staff on a Virgin America flight is not angry, rude, hostile, or overregulated. When your staff has the ability to be genuine and real, it makes a difference to the experience.

The result of all this attention to detail was that Virgin America's inaugural coast-to-coast flights gathered rave reviews from people who had taken the flights. Whether you look at Virgin America or any of the other Virgin brands, they all challenge conventions and stand apart in some way. It really is the perfect brand example to start helping you understand what your organization's personality is because it is unique, authentic, and talkable—the key elements of personality.

Isn't Personality in the Eye of the Beholder?

Building on these elements, the rest of this chapter will introduce you to a framework for personality through something that I call the *UAT Filter*. First, though, we need to address what some might consider a flaw in the idea of defining something as indefinable and broad as personality. If you equate having a personality with a quality like being beautiful, it would be impossible for any study to break down the idea of beauty into neat categories or quantifiable standards in order to determine whether something or someone was beautiful or not. Ideals based on human emotion are all like that.

Personality when referring to an organization, as I mentioned earlier, is different. The personality of an organization is not a combination of character traits like it is for individuals. To return to the definition I shared earlier: **Personality is the unique, authentic, and talkable soul of your brand that people can get passionate about.**

GO TO GUIDE p.257

The three elements of personality noted above are chosen very deliberately: personality requires all three, and the way to look at them is operating together as a filter. Personality does not have to be a subjective idea

left up to each person's sensibilities to define. Before you can hel[
organization get more personality, there needs to be a common framework
for describing it. That's the goal of the UAT Filter.

At first glance, this may seem a bit formulaic as a framework for something as creative and different as a personality. The thing to remember about this particular simplification is that it is not a scientific model; it is a creative one. That's why the word *formula* doesn't really work. "Filter" is much better. A filter is a sequential way of getting to an end result that fits certain criteria. A filter usually also indicates quality. The best water

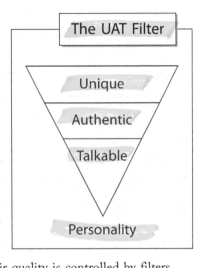

is pure filtered. Vodka is too. Even air quality is controlled by filters.

In terms of defining your brand personality, the best way to think about uniqueness, authenticity, and talkability is to regard them as filters that build upon one another. Every brand used as an example in this book can be put through the UAT filter to identify the core elements of its personality. In addition, the filter provided a model for identifying the right brands and messages to include in this book.

The reason why this filter should be the place where you start is that personality can be easily confused with other things, including marketing campaigns or product design. If you look at the three core elements of personality, all are themes in marketing that you will find lots of resources and advice devoted to. The problem is, most businesses and businesspeople are taught to focus on these elements separately.

GO TO GUIDE *p.* **258**

When you do that, however, you end up with something different. Before we begin to discuss how you can use the UAT filter to define your organization's own personality, let me share a word of caution about another marketing tactic that will be tempting to consider as you seek to define a personality for your organization—the marketing stunt.

Anatomy of a Stunt Marketer

A stunt is usually the enactment of a big idea that involves something highly visual and unique. Having spent most of my career working in an agency helping all kinds of marketing teams promote their products, I know that focusing solely on the stunt is one of the most common mistakes marketers make. Stunts are fun to watch and can often become viral and spread from person to person. Unfortunately, they are also often ideas that are run in the absence of real strategy and have uncertain outcomes.

I don't mean to sound negative about using stunts for marketing, because when used correctly, they can be very effective at attracting notice. The main problem with stunts, though, is that they often will raise eyebrows and obtain momentary notice, but then the bump disappears. Of course, some stunts like Taco Bell's famous April Fools' Day prank in 1996, when they issued a press release saying they had purchased the Liberty Bell in Philadelphia and renamed it the Taco Liberty Bell (inciting letters of complaint to the government until the "announcement" was revealed as a prank), are remembered for a long time. But the connection to the brand is minimal and weak.

Stunts are designed to make impressions. They are limited in scope and often fleeting. To really use your personality for marketing, it needs to go deeper than a stunt. You need to be able to separate having a personality from having a few great marketing stunt ideas. This is the difference between having a real strategy and a collection of tactics. Tactics are executions meant to promote your products or service. Personality offers something more deeply connected to your brand.

To make sure you are focusing on your personality instead of stunts, you need a framework to help you evaluate your ideas, so you can predict what will make an impact. The intention of the UAT Filter is to give you that framework so you can evaluate your ideas and choose the right ones. Often, the problem is not one of having ideas for what to do, but getting direction to help identify where to focus your efforts.

Let's get started by talking about the first element of the filter—being unique.

Street Food Is Unique. . .Sometimes

People travel from all around the world to Chowpatty Beach in Mumbai, India, to sample a type of street food called bhelpuri. A mix of puffed rice, potatoes, onions, chili, mint, coriander, and chutney, the spicy snack is so much of a staple at this popular location in Mumbai that many even consider it the one dining experience in Mumbai not to be missed. Clearly, the bhelpuris on the beach are a unique draw for the city, so it may come as a surprise when I tell you that this is not what I mean by creating a unique experience. The problem with bhelpuris is that once you get to Chowpatty Beach, there are dozens of vendors all selling the same thing. They are not all exactly the same, but you would need to be a very experienced bhelpurist to discern the differences among them. When everyone sells the same "unique" thing, it is nearly impossible to stand out.

Contrast this with an entirely different type of street food served by a guy in a trailer at Woolloomooloo wharf in Sydney, Australia, near an old naval yard. This destination, called Harry's Café de Wheels, is a local legend that opened just after World War II. Harry's serves meat pies loaded with mashed peas and gravy, or hot dogs piled high with toppings. The trailer is right by the water, open late, and most of the patrons eat standing on the curbside because there is no place to sit. No one else does what Harry's does—and his curbside café has been doing it for more than 50 years. Harry's is unique.

Go to just about any other city in the world and you will see the same kind of thing. Climax Jerky is a business based in a buffalo wagon outside the Silverthorne outlet shopping center in Colorado selling every type of jerky imaginable. Voodoo Doughnuts is another iconic local favorite in Portland, Oregon, which markets itself as the best-tasting donut in the world (created from the secret recipes of "donut masters" from Pico Rivera, California), and described as the choice of "artists, actors, washed up sports stars, old people, disillusioned tourists, and musicians." Unique finds like these often define the places they come from, or vice versa. They are the local legends that inspire people to have new experiences that they could not have anywhere else. There is one city that seems to inspire more of these unique destinations than others, because of how it chooses to describe itself: weird.

The residents of Austin, Texas, like to note their location in the heart of conservative Texas as an ironic coincidence. The city brands itself as the "Live Music Capital of the World" and with the internationally famous South by Southwest (SxSW) music, film, and interactive festival taking place there every March and T-shirts all over the city imploring visitors and residents alike to "Keep Austin Weird," it is easy to see how it could live up to its self-inscribed reputation. One Austin resident doing his part to help is Steve Busti, the owner of a gift shop called the Lucky Lizard.

The Lucky Lizard stands out as one of the few retail destinations on Sixth Street that is not a bar or a restaurant. Steve describes his shop as being all about carrying unique, one-of-a-kind gifts, many of which are created by local artists. To further the cult of weird, Steve also used the back of his store to open what he calls the Museum of the Weird. The store within his store features shrunken heads and other assorted freaky knickknacks. In a weird city, Lucky Lizard offers a stage for the weirdness and a way of taking a piece of it home with you.

From meat pies on the streets of Sydney to the Museum of the Weird in Austin, there are thousands of unique travel destinations everywhere around the world. The lessons they offer include not only how to create something unique, but also how to use the first element of the filter to put your brand on a track toward acquiring personality. Being unique is the first step.

How to Be Unique

Street food and travel experiences offer many wonderful examples of how to be unique. Beyond signatures or stunts, there are four true methods for creating something unique.

1. **Find the Uncontested Space.** This is the most reliable, but most difficult, method. It involves finding a business that no one else is in, and then defining it through your company. It is also the hardest to rely on, because as soon as you create a new industry there will be other challengers entering and ready to take you on. Priceline and eBay have both managed to do this online. Nintendo's Wii, Cirque du Soleil, and Crocs are all examples of others that have created a new niche for themselves by forging into new areas to make their competition irrelevant.

2. **Position Yourself.** Positioning is the art of defining how you want to be perceived without necessarily changing the product you have. From the citizens of Halfway, Oregon, renaming their town to Half.com in 1999 for the notoriety of being the first real town

to be named after a dot-com, to a small town in Romania called Sighişoara that proudly proclaims itself the birthplace of Vlad Ţepeş (the prince who inspired the Count Dracula stories)—the art of positioning uniquely is alive and well in small towns around the world. Ultimately, this is closely linked to storytelling—a topic we will explore fully in Chapter 4.

3. **Create a Twist.** Many times, you will be in a business where finding that completely different position seems impossible. In these businesses, you need to find an element that is unique and ownable that sets you apart. This is the twist. Finding this twist can be tricky because it should be about more than just finding your "signature service." It needs to be more significant. Introducing a new variety of Coke, for example, is not a significant enough twist. On the other hand, Fadó Irish Pub opened in 1996 in Atlanta and featured furniture and stones for the exterior of the bar directly from Ireland and created a unique experience that stood apart from all the other bars in the popular Buckhead area of Atlanta. That was their twist.

4. **Think Outside Your Region.** This is not about changing your business, but about changing where you do it. If you have a regional business that is the same as that of several competitors, consider uprooting and establishing it elsewhere. This is not possible for everyone, but for those who have the option, it can offer a strong way to stand out. A single bhelpuri vendor on the streets of Manhattan would stand out. There is a restaurant in Washington, D.C., called Cassatt's that is the only place in the city where you can get a flat white (a popular espresso-based coffee drink similar to a latte and served mainly in Australia and New Zealand). Bringing a regional experience

to an unexpected place and doing it in a way indistinguishable from the "real thing" makes Cassatt's unique.

As you know by now, being unique is only the first (and arguably the easiest) of the three elements of personality. So far, many of the examples for unique businesses have focused on one particular type of industry—restaurants and travel destinations. Let's broaden our focus and start to talk about the second element that influences how your personality is truly shaped and how your customer's perception of your business is formed—authenticity.

Transparency Is Overrated

Being the only one on the block to sell something will take you only so far. Authenticity can be the hook that takes you from simply offering something different to building trust with your customers. Of course, as I shared earlier in the book, the word *authenticity* is rapidly becoming a cliché in business today. Part of the reason is that we live in a world where authenticity is often and easily faked. The examples of brands faking authenticity today abound and are increasingly familiar to people. Häagen-Dazs, Foster's, and Bombay Company are just a few examples of brands built upon the claim of a global heritage, but whose roots are solely and distinctly American. Every day there are more and more brands that try to claim authenticity through creative branding. They all want to be authentic.

The main reason why "authenticity" is such a buzzword right now, though, does not have to do with where products come from, but with the changing way that businesses communicate with their customers. The most common misperception about authenticity is that it is all about transparency. There are entire manifestos being written about how important transparency is, while government organizations are simultaneously mandating transparency when it comes to financial records and transactions. Isn't this the same as authenticity?

It isn't and here's why. Transparency requires being open about what you are doing and admitting that you are doing it. What's missing is an evaluation about whether what you're doing is right or wrong. If you're transparent about the fact that you don't listen to your customers and are not interested in their opinions, you're not being very authentic even though you are transparent. That's the danger of focusing too much on transparency, and why you should leave it to the lawyers and accountants to figure out what you need to be transparent about and shift your attention to authenticity. Unless, of course, that lawyer happens to be your company's founder.

Authenticity in Every Pocket

The last place anyone would have expected to see a brilliant example of an authentic brand is in a company created by a former lawyer. Scott Jordan was a corporate and real estate lawyer on the usual trajectory out of law school. He worked at a big firm and quickly became used to commuting across the country every week for his job. By every definition of the word, he was what is commonly called a "road warrior." On each of those trips, he would watch business travelers slowly empty their pockets of all the gadgets they owned in the airport security line, and he would think to himself that there must be a better way to carry our ever-increasing bundle of gadgets around with us each day. Inspired by his idea, he founded SCOTTEVEST (SeV) as the first company to produce what he then called "Gear Management Clothing."

In 2001 when Scott first started producing his clothing, gadget overload was just starting to hit. Many men were increasingly carrying around what was derogatorily called the "man purse" and it was not exactly the most masculine of choices. The real problem was that a line of clothing that would allow you to carry around all these gadgets, without making you look like you could win first prize at a geek fashion show at MIT, didn't exist. So Scott and his wife Laura founded a company to create it.

When I got my first vest from SCOTTEVEST, it had 29 pockets. If it sounds like a lot, it is. This was the first piece of clothing I ever owned that I would have to learn how to use. Thankfully, each pocket included a small business card with ideas for what could go into the pocket. The vest also came with a stack of small cards that I could give to friends, along with Scott's personal story.

It is these little touches like the cards in the pockets, or the fact that Scott still personally answers his phone and responds to e-mails directly, that make SCOTTEVEST what it is. It also made it easy to get in touch with Scott to talk to him about the premise for my book. In one particularly telling moment, Scott spoke about the need for his company to scale quickly and attract investors. A part of it was demonstrating how the company was "real" through their Web site. To that end, he described the inside story of adding a fictional member of the management team named Kelly Adoggi. Here is Kelly's corporate profile on the company site:

> Kelly Adoggi is the Director of Marketing of SeV. A recent graduate, Kelly is the product of home schooling and private tutors. Her parents— described by Kelly as "unconventional mavericks"—felt that traditional education would not prepare her for this dog-eat-dog world. They saw in her the ability to take the ball and run with it and, consequently, put her in real life situations to develop her problem-solving skills. Kelly raves about her unique education. A self-described leader of the pack, her only bone to pick with her parents was her lack of classmates. Kelly was very excited when she heard about the position at SeV, as she felt it was something she could really sink

her teeth into. Although her experience was more limited than some applicants, she won Laura and Scott over with her never say die attitude. In her interview, she had Scott in stitches as she explained that she is not one to roll over and play dead—that she will sniff out information with rabid enthusiasm. Kelly's hobbies include hiking, running, walking, sleeping and eating. She is currently working on her first book, a collection of feminist short stories about loyalty and faithfulness tentatively titled, *Every Dog Has Her Day*.

If you haven't figured it out already, Kelly Adoggi is a pseudonym for one of Scott and Laura's dogs—and an inside joke about the company that Scott sometimes shares with customers. I talked earlier about the desire for many small companies to appear big. Some let this desire force them into choices that hide their personalities. Kelly's profile is a great example of how Scott has managed to keep his company authentic while still fulfilling the need to appear at times more established than he was. Recently the company added 12 new employees (including a real director of marketing) and is fielding a rapidly increasing number of orders. His company's personality, however, remains friendly, authentic, and conversational. And yes, Scott still answers the phone.

How to Be Authentic

What Scott Jordan's story shows us is that authentic brands know how to keep their real voices and use them to build credibility and trust with their customers. They have values that their customers share and are honest in their interactions. Honesty, in particular, can be a scary word for brands. For some, it means giving up information that was previously kept secret or refraining from making promises to customers that the brand cannot live up to. For these reasons, authenticity must be built from several key components.

1. **Define a Credible Heritage.** Where a company comes from is a great place to start to build the authentic story behind the brand. Having a real heritage that customers can identify with brings a brand to life and demonstrates that there was a real struggle by real people to start and build the company. As we will explore in Chapter 4, telling this story well is the key to providing the right foundation for your customers and employees, enabling them to believe in your brand.

2. **Demonstrate Passion and Belief.** The real passion behind a company is something that cannot be faked or manipulated, and people easily recognize it when this is being done. Authentic companies have people working there who are passionate about the mission of the organization. When this passion comes through in its interactions with customers, the brand is perceived as far more real and powerful.

3. **Foster Individuals Instead of People.** It is of the utmost importance to have your employees act as individuals rather than as parts of one monolithic and impersonal group. Authentic brands have individuals working for them who are the ones that demonstrate the passion and belief behind the brand—a point we first talked about in Chapter 2.

4. **Have Motives Beyond Profit.** Companies that have an authenticity are also the ones that focus on goals beyond short-term profit. This criterion includes the idea of good and bad profits, as well as of authentic and inauthentic motives. If a customer

feels like every interaction with you is nothing more than a chance for you to sell something, trust erodes. If, on the other hand, the interactions are about something more than profit, you can build trust.

You are almost there, but if you are only focused on being unique and authentic—you will have a great story but with hardly anyone telling it. The last element of the UAT filter is all about amplifying your personality and making it visible. In traditional marketing terms, if you think of finding your unique element as positioning and interacting authentically as the way to build trust and credibility, then talkability is the all-important final component of personality. It allows your brand to travel from person to person and manifest the benefits of positive word of mouth.

How Talkability Relates to WOM

Just about every piece of marketing advice you get these days will repeat the same obvious truth—word of mouth is the most influential source of trusted advice for most consumers. At one time, it was easy for brands to think of word of mouth as an add-on effect that happened outside of your marketing, almost beyond your control. What pioneering WOM thinkers like Andy Sernovitz and Ed Keller have been illustrating through their books[1] and work with the Word of Mouth Marketing Association (WOMMA) is that there is a way to foster word of mouth and help it happen for your products and brand *on purpose*. Word of mouth doesn't have to be an accidental phenomenon.

Talkability is the third part of the UAT filter for a reason. It ties the idea of personality back to the core benefits of word-of-mouth market-

[1] *Word of Mouth Marketing* (Sernovitz) and *The Influentials* (Keller).

ing. Talkability is the hook that makes someone want to share your message with her or his friends and family. Creating something talkable is all about finding the right hook and helping your customers pass it on.

The reason this can often be difficult is that achieving talkability requires a type of thinking that many brands are not prepared for because the "sell" is not your product but the talkable message that someone is likely to pass on to someone else. Imagine you have a new DVD for a documentary film that you want to distribute. Consider two approaches you could take. The first is to identify the demographics of your target audience, find the media that they read, and place advertising or PR messages there. This is what most marketers would do.

The second approach is to find the much smaller group of people who would be interested in the film and also highly inclined to tell 10, 15, or 50 others about it. Then you give each of them two copies for free, one for them to keep and the other to give someone else. The talkability of that approach means your film will get in front of many more people and eventually you will sell it to people who you never anticipated (assuming it is good and people recommend it—don't forget that personality can't make a bad idea better).

What Dave Matthews Knows about Buzz

This focus on recommendations is also the secret behind the viral success of the Dave Matthews Band (DMB). When I was living in Atlanta in the mid-1990s, DMB was just a popular college band that did shows at small venues and had a big college fan base, including a fellow who lived in my college dorm.

On his shelf were hundreds of bootlegged cassette tapes (yes, it was back when people still used tapes) and each was of a different show by the Dave Matthews Band as it played across the United States. At each show, there were cover songs, different versions of some of their favorite songs, and real concert moments. Each was a unique experience and collecting them made you feel like part of the band. What DMB realized early was that giving their most involved fans the freedom to tape and distribute their shows was the ultimate way to create their own army of ambassadors for their music. The experience of listening to any of these shows was immediately talkable because you were sharing in a unique moment. DMB was a live band in the truest sense of the word, every one of their shows was different and had unique moments.

That unique experience is what I remember about the band (and what I still tell others about it). Though they have now become "mainstream," I still associate them with those scratchy bootleg cassettes that I listened to in my college dorm room just over a decade ago.

How to Be Talkable

How did DMB create something so talkable that it kept fans engaged for more than a decade and helped propel them from a college band to mega-superband status? For one thing, they demonstrated a strong understanding of the following core lessons:

1. **Offer something of value and that is limited.** By letting their fans tape and share shows, DMB had a built-in distribution channel that would ensure that their music spread from person to person. Having a very different sound certainly helped (as they were unique), but letting these show recordings travel offered fans some ownership of discovering the band. It also provided the incentive to share—which is the most important benefit of offering something of value.

2. **Have a hook that is shareable.** The hook is the factor that gets people talking. It is the thing that makes your brand or product interesting and worthy of discussion. For DMB, it was the composition of the band (they have the normal guitar, bass, and drummer—as well as a violin player and a sax player), as well as Dave himself and his wildly difficult guitar riffs that went way beyond the typical three-chord guitar riffs that many other alternative bands of the time were using to create their hit songs.

3. **Get out of the way.** This may seem like the strangest strategy of all, but sometimes it is the best one. Consumers want to share their opinions and discuss things they are passionate about. If there is a vibrant discussion happening already and it is on your message, the best thing you can do is step back and let it happen.

So now that we have learned about the different elements of the UAT filter, it is time to put all the pieces together and start using it. To learn how, let's start by looking at the case study of a company that took the idea of a local grocery store and infused it with a human tradition that people have been engaging in for thousands of years: trading.

A Trader That Breaks All the Rules

Imagine that part of your job involved tasting 12 types of dark chocolate from around the world to find the perfect one to sell? There are people whose jobs involve this type of tasting, but they are not usually among the regular employees at a company. They are most often wine or food critics or people who are writing some type of commentary on food and beverages. At Trader Joe's, these tasters are the employees and their qualification is that they are real people just like their customers.

As Jeff Caporizzo, a former senior art director with Trader Joe's, notes:

> No matter what department you worked in, you could look forward
> to tasting an assortment of fine chocolates, jumbo shrimp, nutty soy-
> milk or other tasty submissions. It brought us together as co-workers
> and exemplified the personality of the company. . .a place where
> FOOD comes first and we would stop a workday, get together, eat
> and talk about the experience.

Traders thousands of years ago pioneered a particular model of commerce that didn't involve money, but instead giving someone one item in exchange for another. It was the ultimate trust deal, sealed with a handshake and built on a collection of personal experiences. More than 40 years ago, Trader Joe's was opened as a new kind of grocery store founded on principles inspired by those of the early traders. The main principle was that every product sold in the store was tasted and selected by a member of their buying team.

As a result, walking into the store is like walking into the pantry of a good friend and seeing a range of products selected with you in mind. The store publishes catalogs full of products like Mojito Salmon (fresh frozen Atlantic-grade salmon with a signature mojito sauce) and it sells the majority of its products, sourced from producers around the world, under its own brand name. The Trader Joe's Web site describes the mission of the company:

> We travel the world in search of interesting, unique, great-tasting
> foods and beverages. We buy direct from the producer whenever pos-
> sible. We strip away all the fancy stuff and focus on the important
> things like natural ingredients and inspiring flavors. We run a pretty

lean ship, too—you won't find any corporate jets or fancy offices around here. Heck, our CEO doesn't even have a secretary!

And what does our fanatical frugality do for you? It guarantees you the best values you can find anywhere around on the best foods and beverages we can find from everywhere around the world.

Among the myriad supermarkets and grocery stores housing countless faceless aisles of mass-produced food, Trader Joe's has pioneered a different experience that customers rave about. Along the way, the company has broken just about every traditional rule of the grocery business. Their stores are smaller and do not waste real estate on the wide aisles that their largest competitors say are a requirement. They take liberties with their brand, changing their name and logo from Trader Joe's to Trader Giotto's for products if it fits better. They carry relatively few fruits and vegetables, ensuring that they will not fit the mold of a "one-stop shop."

In a sea of the same experiences, Trader Joe's is unique and stands apart. It has a mix of a diverse range of products, an authentic brand identity, and an experience that consumers can't help telling one another about. From the plastic lobsters (there's one in every store) to its focus on selling products that have all been taste-tested and specially purchased to be sold at Trader Joe's, the experience of visiting a store is less like a chore and more like an adventure.

The Personality Principles

When it comes to Trader Joe's or Oil Can Henry's—the common elements that unite these brands is an understanding of how to use personality to stand out, and their focus on something that is more than a signature. Across the first three chapters of this book, we have seen how and why brands lose personality, how accidental spokespeople are starting to help brands tell stories and rediscover their personalities, and now have the framework to understand the personality behind your brand and how to define it. When it comes to putting that personality into action, there are three core principles you need to know.

1. **Principle 1: Talk like a real person.** Avoid clichés or a form of writing or what is affectionately known to businesspeople as "marketingspeak." The purpose of talking like a real person is one that was first introduced in Chapter 1: to build credibility. Using a conversational style of communication is one of the cornerstones of personality and a necessity for any brand.

2. **Principle 2: Admit you are marketing.** Guess what? Your customers already know what you're trying to do. Admitting that you are marketing addresses the "elephant in the room" and demonstrates that you are willing to be honest about what you are up to. You have a product or service you think someone would be interested in, they have their attention as currency that they can either give to you or not. Ironically, the admission that you are marketing can often create a compelling reason for a customer to pay attention, as long as your message is relevant.

3. **Principle 3. Have a sense of humor.** Faceless companies never laugh. They have inane policies and laughable marketing proclamations but are loath to poke fun at themselves. Companies that can do this automatically win credibility for being more authentic and real. This is not about turning everything into a joke or always making people laugh, however. Humor has to be appropriate, but having it is an essential element.

The UAT filter is all about positioning and how you define your organization. Remembering these principles will help you as we move from talking about positioning your brand and finding the right spokespeople into actually putting personality into action. The next chapter focuses on how to create a backstory for your brand that your customers can believe in.

The Sellevator Pitch

The personality of your organization is the combination of what is unique, authentic, and talkable about it. The UAT Filter helps you identify your personality by looking at these elements sequentially.

Chapter 4

Lessons from the Storytellers
Crafting a Backstory People Care About

Did you know that every banana has an untold story? It is not that anyone tries to keep it a secret, but as most bananas make their journey from the farm where they were grown to the local store near you, the story behind how they arrived there is usually lost. Most fruits are like this, making their way anonymously from around the world to your local market. Fruit is faceless.

If you are like most people, you probably just pick up your bananas, make sure they are not overripe or dented, and then buy them. Bananas are commodity products. You don't have a deep emotional attachment to bananas, you are just buying something you need. This is the problem with commodity products: they are low involvement. When you have a product like this, how can you differentiate yourself from your competitors, who make almost exactly the same thing? You might argue that taste or quality is the way to stand out, but who can really taste the difference between two of the same variety of bananas? Remember, we're talking about a low-involvement product here.

There *is* one interesting fact about bananas, though, that makes them different from many other fruits. People have some brand associations with bananas, which means they are not as completely faceless as other fruits may be. Chiquita, Dole, and Del Monte are all household names of brands that sell bananas. Why do bananas have these brand associations while most other fruits don't? Chiquita deserves much of the credit for this, as they were the first to start branding bananas back in the 1940s with an iconic brand character called Miss Chiquita, a catchy jingle, and recognizable stickers on all its bananas. At a time when most fruit was sold anonymously, these stickers were a big deal. They attached a brand to a commodity product and made people aware that they were buying a *Chiquita* banana.

For decades, Miss Chiquita kept Chiquita at the top of the banana category, but then in the 1970s Chiquita's market share started to slip for a variety of reasons, including the EU Banana Regime of 1993.[1] Nearly a decade later, another series of events and small controversies led to Chiquita filing for Chapter 11 bankruptcy and opened the door further for competitors to gain even more ground. Today, Miss Chiquita is still the face of the brand, but the company is fighting several legal battles, facing a fading brand relevancy, and suffering a loss of its market share to Dole, the company's biggest competitor.

What allowed Chiquita to rule the banana market for decades was not just its ability to produce bananas people liked (most producers can do that), but its ability to put the recognizable face of Miss Chiquita on them. The reason for the slippage, as we might have expected with this icon based on what we learned in Chapter 2, is that with a character spokesperson there are some real limitations in a world where con-

---

[1]This is a really interesting story, but not really relevant to marketing. To see the full story, search Google for "EU Banana Regime."

sumers are demanding more authenticity. Miss Chiquita is no longer enough. But could any other brand really do better than her to create an emotional bond between a consumer and something as perishable as a banana?

Bringing Bananas to Life

Dole has found an innovative answer to this question by connecting their customers to a very unlikely place, a farm called Don Pedro located deep in the arid plains of La Guajira in northern Colombia. This farm, like hundreds of others like it, is part of Dole's Certified Organic Banana Program. There are real farmers working on this farm, living real lives that are affected by the way that they interact with Dole and grow the bananas that the company ships around the world. In itself, this arrangement is not unique; however, what usually happens is that the human story behind the growing, picking, packaging, and shipping of fruit is lost as the fruit travels from a real farm somewhere in the world to a two-level display unit in a grocery store in suburbia.

Dole has found a way to humanize this scenario. Each banana produced as part of Dole's program has a three-digit "farm code" printed on it that allows anyone to go online and see details about the farm that grew the banana. As Frans Wielemaker, director of sourcing for Dole describes it, the program was built to "increase transparency and thus consumer confidence." The Certified Organic Banana Program brought the story behind Dole's bananas to life in a much more powerful way than any fictional character wearing bananas on her head ever did.

Proof of the results of the program came in a small way in June 2007, when Dole published the following excerpted letter to the employees of Don Pedro Farm (and their response) on the companion blog to the program.

05/24/2007 12:58 PM
From: Amanda Shepard
Country: USA

Comments: Thank you for what you are doing. Thank you for giving consumers the opportunity to provide aid and hope with our choices. Thank you also for this site that allows us to get a glimpse of the lives of those growing the bananas and the beautiful land on which the bananas are grown. I will think of the people and the beautiful landscape at Don Pedro Farm every time I eat a Dole organic banana. Be so proud of what you are doing!

To: Amanda Shepard
With all our appreciation: Finca Don Pedro, Colombia
Ms. Shepard:

Today, at 6:05 AM, I personally read your e-mail to all our employees in Don Pedro Farm in La Guajira Colombia. They are very happy and very proud about your words. It was a different way to start their working day, somebody from a foreign country, thousands of miles north of their home town sending a beautiful and inspiring message to them, was reason enough to consider today as their better day at work ever.

Luis Monge, Organic Program, DFFI

The rest of this blog post features real responses from more than a dozen workers at Don Pedro Farm, including photos of each worker and a personal note of thanks. It is a powerful testimonial to Dole's authenticity and its decision to show the consumer there are real people who are affected by the purchase decisions we all make. The farm codes and these stories humanize the bananas from Dole, and provide a reason for customers to care about the brand sticker on their bananas. Buying a Dole banana now means that you are helping to support these real people in Colombia who grow them. It is now an emotional choice as much as a practical one. This is the power of creating a compelling *backstory;* it can give your customers a reason to believe in your brand beyond the products or services themselves.

The Real Power of the Backstory

A backstory is the history behind an organization and how it became what it is today. It is not a timeline of accomplishments or the boilerplate history that can often be found on company Web sites. The backstory is something more meaningful. It has real characters and a believable tale of how these characters had to evolve and overcome challenges in order to make their business successful. In Dole's case, this backstory is the real story of the many people who work together to grow, package, and ship their bananas around the world. Forget the old ideas of publishing a company history or even an "about us" page on a Web site. This chapter will offer you a new way to think about how you describe where your company comes from.

Using stories to bring brands or products to life is not a new idea. There are many models describing how marketing can be influenced by storytelling principles. Books like *Made to Stick, All Marketers Are Liars,* and *The Elements of Persuasion* are all, to some degree, about storytelling. Each offers a smart point of view about the elements of a story, how to craft one that works, and the triggers that make stories memorable. So what's different about a backstory?

Stories help marketers to put product benefits or values into emotional terms, which is a key ingredient in a backstory. What is different about a backstory is that its only goal is to create a foundation of credibility. It is not about putting product virtues into human terms or telling a story that may persuade someone to purchase something. Though a credible story may influence purchase, the best way to think about the backstory is this: If telling stories about your product or service is the main dish in your marketing meal, then creating a backstory is the appetizer.

The backstory is the foundation from which you can build your business. In Chapter 3, we learned about the model for understanding the personality by using the UAT Filter. Recall that the first principle of personality we discussed is to have a human voice. To use that voice for crafting your backstory, the first step is to master the rhythm of dialogue (the one thing many marketers forget to do).

Your Marketing Is Not the *Titanic* (We Hope)

To understand dialogue, screenwriting is a good place to start. Not that every movie has mastered the art of realistic human dialogue (we'll see a tragic example of where it goes wrong a bit later), but screenwriting and the related art of playwriting are forms that are meant to capture the distinctive rhythm of human dialogue. Lines in a screenplay or play are written to be spoken out loud, not read silently.

As an exercise to show how your marketing writing is unlike natural human dialogue, I want you to try a simple experiment. Take the first few lines of your company's "about us" description from your Web site or any other printed materials and force yourself to read it out loud. By the way, make sure you are alone because most likely you are about to sound like a fool. Can you imagine anyone ever saying those lines in

GO TO GUIDE p. 269 a real conversation? Is that how you describe your company to strangers? If it wasn't before, it is probably now painfully obvious to you that the way in which companies describe themselves and their history is often indecipherable. You need to lose the buzzwords.

No one knows this better than Brian Fugere. Brian is a consultant with Deloitte Consulting and a self-described "jargonaholic." In 2003, Deloitte offered a tool to clients called the "Bullfighter," which plugged into Microsoft Word and PowerPoint. It measures the number of jargon words and generates a score called the "Bull Composite Index." The Bullfighter was a viral success, and the tool and philosophy behind it even inspired a book called *Why Business People Speak Like Idiots*. In the book, Brian and his coauthors describe this change:

> There is a gigantic disconnect between these real, authentic conversations and the artificial voice of business executives and managers at every level. Their messages lack humanity in a world that craves more of it. Between meetings, memos, and managers, we've lost the art of conversation. Bull has become the language of business.

Even screenwriters lapse into their share of "bull"; however, for a screenwriter it is usually called a cliché. A good example of losing the rhythm of dialogue comes from a string of pain-inducing clichés from the aptly named movie, *Titanic*.

1. "A woman's heart is a deep ocean of secrets."
2. "Our love was endless like the ocean."
3. "He saved me in every way that a person can be saved."
4. "He exists now, only in my memory."

Okay, I made up one of these four lines—but I bet you can't tell which one.[2] The movie was filled with lines like this and as a result the dialogue suffered. It wasn't real. But it did win lots of awards and make hundreds of millions of dollars. So if it did so well, how can I use it as an example of something that doesn't work? Simple—because my point is about being real and authentic.

When you go to see a movie like *Titanic,* what you are buying is melodrama and special effects in the form of entertainment. You know this before you walk into the theater, so the movie would have been a failure if it didn't deliver on both. Clearly, it did, and ended up thanking the Academy a record 11 times for the awards the film took home in 1997. The lesson in this is unless your business is selling melodrama, do not let your marketing sound like the dialogue in *Titanic.*

Backstories and the Dharma Initiative

Lost is a television show that features a group of survivors of a plane crash trapped on an island and battling for their survival while trying to solve the many mysteries they are confronted with. One of those mysteries is the secretive Dharma Initiative, which was once a settlement on the island. Of course, finding characters in overly dramatic situations that they must fight their way out of is nothing new in television, right? Yet as any fan of the show will tell you, it is the unique narrative model focused on the backstory through flashbacks (and "flashforwards") that J.J. Abrams created for the series that has as much as anything else been a large part of the show's success and loyal following. The show attracts more than 16 million viewers per episode and a survey of 20 countries by Informa Telecoms and Media in 2006 concluded that *Lost* was the second most viewed TV show in the world (after *CSI: Miami*).

[2]The second one is made up. Several recent scientific studies have uncovered that the ocean isn't actually endless.

The power of *Lost* is that it took this standard on-screen convention in television and movies, and expanded it with a new idea: focusing an entire episode on one character's backstory. Each subsequent episode of the show focused on another character. The resulting format offered a fast-paced forward and backward look at each character in the show, one per week. The format allowed viewers to more deeply bond with each character, and decide whether or not they liked her or him, because the viewer spent an entire hour (minus commercials) watching a story about a character's past intertwined with the present action, which gave each character depth.

Lessons from Lost—*Why a Backstory Works*

- Provides more reasons to care about each character.
- Offers context for characters' current actions.
- Creates mystery by allowing audience to know details that characters themselves do not.

The challenge with any story is to create empathy, and *Lost* has met this challenge by its use of the backstory. Empathy means that the audience relates somehow to the main character and cares what happens to him or her. This is not about liking a character. It is possible to like someone but not care about what happens to her or him and to care deeply about a flawed character who is not necessarily likeable. Creating empathy is about building an emotional investment in a character, so that viewers will care about what happens to this character regardless of whether or not they like the character. Getting an audience to go from complete unfamiliarity to empathy means you need to establish hooks in a character's story very early. Here is a quick fictional example.

A single dad who is also working is shown in an early scene singing to his daughter over the phone to put her to sleep as he is stuck at a shift job at a desk late at night. You see on his face that it pains him that he's not there—while around him you see mounds of papers stacked up that he clearly still needs to go through before he can leave.

The premise established in less than 10 seconds: he's a good but overworked father. Now as a viewer you're emotionally invested in him. You want him to succeed, even though you don't know anything about him or the situation he will soon face. That's how rapid character development works. Now let's focus on how this applies to your business.

Thinking Like a Screenwriter

The lesson in the success of *Lost* is that the backstory works as a tool to build an emotional connection. This is why crafting a backstory is the important first element in demonstrating the personality of your brand. Of course, the format I describe above works great for television and movies, but how does it apply to marketing and promoting your business?

This is not about telling a visual message on screen. It is important, however, to tell your story *visually*. To understand this point, let's consider a few of the things that good screenwriters must do.

1. Establish characters and stories quickly.
2. Create scenes and moments rather than prose and descriptions.
3. Always write with natural human language.
4. Foster an emotional connection with no basis of knowledge.
5. Weave these elements into a compelling story with a beginning, middle, and end.

Sound familiar? The challenges are no different than those you face in telling your backstory. The mediums are different, as your end goal is not necessarily to create something watchable on a screen, but you must establish your characters and story to foster an emotional connection. You need to think like a screenwriter.

The BArc Model

The *story arc* is a common phrase used to describe the changes that happen to a main character from the beginning to the end of any story (not just a screenplay). It goes from low points to high points, while introducing conflict to raise the stakes of the story. When it comes to applying these conventions of storytelling to your backstory, the best way to approach it is to use something called the Backstory Arc (BArc).

The BArc is the progression that your backstory must take in order to build an emotional investment. There are five key elements in the BArc Model.

- **Characters**—Who are the people in the story that your customers must associate with?
- **Challenge**—What is the key question or need they are trying to answer?
- **Vision**—What was the unique idea or premise that they embarked upon?
- **Conflict**—Who or what stands in the way of their success?
- **Triumph**—How are they (or will they) overcome this conflict?

To create a successful backstory for your brand, you must always *address* these five elements (though you don't always need to have an answer for each).

In researching the many types of backstories that are presented by companies, it became clear that several specific types of backstories are repeated over and over again. When I first discovered this, I went looking for a model for these stories in one of the hundreds of marketing or business books on my office shelf, and found none. I did, however, find a similar insight about story patterns in a brilliant book about screenwriting, by screenwriter Blake Snyder, called *Save the Cat!*

Snyder breaks down just about every Hollywood film into 12 distinct story types and maps out for the aspiring screenwriter how to create a story in each type. The pattern that emerged from my research into many company backstories can be summed up in five key models that you should consider as you start to craft your own backstory. The rest of this chapter is dedicated to taking you through these five types of stories, showing you examples of who uses each type, and helping you to determine which may be right one for your organization.

How to Use the Backstory Model Picker

GO TO
GUIDE
*p.*259

To help you get started, there is a tool called the Backstory Model Picker in Part Two that can help you choose among these five models. As you will see as you read through the picker, most backstories actually draw upon elements from multiple models. For this reason, the tool is meant to help you choose a primary story model. As you delve more deeply into your particular organization, you may find that the other models offer supporting evidence or other story elements worth using as well.

Alternatively, you might find that a single story model is ideal without any support from another model. Either way, the chart below should help you to compare and contrast the different story models, and focus on the one that makes the most sense for your business.

Backstory Type	What's the Story?	Who Use
The Passionate Enthusiast	A driven individual takes a personal passion and builds it into a successful business.	• MOO.com (this chapter) • Storyville Coffee (this chapter) • Moleskine (Chapter 2)
The Inspired Inventor	A tireless inventor creates something new and different by not giving up on his/her vision.	• Dyson Vacuums (this chapter) • Molecular Gastronomy (this chapter) • Apple (Chapter 1)
The Smart Listener	A new company is created as a result of listening to customers, partners, or others.	• Google (this chapter) • Stacy's Chips (this chapter) • Dell (Chapter 5)
The Likeable Hero	A dedicated individual overcomes all odds to make his/her idea work.	• Kiva.org (this chapter) • Mission Bay Community Church (this chapter) • Innocent Drinks (Chapter 6)

4

(continued on page 114)

(continued from page 113)

Backstory Type	What's the Story?	Who Uses It?
The Little Guy vs. the Big Guy	An underdog company takes on a seemingly unbeatable, established adversary.	• Under Armour (this chapter) • Bugaboo Strollers (this chapter) • Oil Can Henry's (Chapter 3)

To better understand the five types of backstories and which may make sense in relation to your company's situation, and how it can help you build a foundation of credibility for your brand, let's explore some examples of each type of backstory and some brands that are using them. For each type, there is an associated guide in Part Two that shows how you can use the BArc Model to craft that particular type of story for your business.

Passionate Enthusiast Story: The Cure for Printing Paralysis

Do you suffer from *printing paralysis*? This is a brilliantly descriptive term that I first encountered during a brainstorming session at which someone described the increasingly common trend of people no longer printing their digital photos (in effect, "trapping" them on the computer). The rise of digital photography has all but displaced film, and many of the children born in the last five years will never even know a time when cameras used film. The downside of this move to everything digital is that more and more people are just sharing images online and never printing them out. The satisfaction of holding a printed photo in your hands, or creating a physical photo album or scrapbook is slowly becoming a rare thing.

Yet these physical interactions with the images of our lives still have a certain magic associated with them. When you hold a print in your hands or share it with someone else in a physical way, it makes it more real. There is a corresponding pleasure in seeing your image that you created printed onto a product, or a card, or a T-shirt, or just about anything else you can imagine. MOO.com is a company that was originally created to help you have more of those magic moments.

The first time I heard of MOO was at a conference where a colleague handed me what he called his MOOCard. It was a half-sized business card printed on a beautiful coated card stock and had a full-color image taken by my colleague on one side of it. Clearly this was done by someone who knew printing. I later learned that someone turned out to be Richard Moross, an entrepreneur based in London who saw a worldwide market for a new type of business card with personality. As his team describes it on their site:

> Our first product, MiniCards, came about when we realized that sometimes, we wanted to hand out details of our personal sites, and we just didn't have a nice way to do it. A business card was too cheesy, too serious, or too. . .businessy, and didn't represent us the way we really are. A hastily scribbled piece of paper is more personal, but who ever has paper or a pen when you want it? We needed something else.

The MiniCards were born and became a sensation among fast movers and new media mavens. The cards were profiled in top blogs like Boing Boing, Cool Hunting, GigaOm, and in a *BusinessWeek* article. They were even described as the "unbusiness card of choice at many new media unconferences."[3] By using smart linking with existing social media sites like Flickr and Facebook to let people upload their images, Moo has created a series of tools that make printing fun and necessary again. The passion they have for printing has awakened the same passion among many of their customers.

The partnership with Flickr is perhaps the one place where the passion of Moo customers (or the MOOvment as they are collectively known) is most visibly on display. Some customers collect cards, while others create wall-sized posters out of them. There are photos of one user who sewed a "MOOPocket," which she now sells to keep your cards in, and another user (a teacher) demonstrates how she uses the cards as index cards to teach her class. There are even groups of people who have started collecting and trading MOOCards with one another. MOO may have started as a labor of love from printing enthusiasts, but it has quickly grown to create a community based on people who have similar passions.

Passionate Enthusiast Story: Saving the World— One Cup at a Time

Storyville Coffee is another company founded by passionate enthusiasts, and describes its mission as "saving the world, one cup at a time." Storyville's method of saving the world has to do with first saving all of us from bad coffee, which they only half jokingly refer to as "acid rain." For Storyville, its backstory comes down to first changing people's perceptions of coffee by sharing two facts.

1. Coffee expires because it has natural oils.
2. Most coffee is burned to get rid of oils and help it last longer.

[3] "A Business Card for Your Avatar" http://www.businessweek.com/smallbiz/content/jul2007/sb2007076_772566_page_2.htm

Storyville's coffee, unlike many others, has an expiration date. The company also offers only two varieties (regular and decaf), which means you will still have to get your caramel mint pumpkin spiced skim decaf no-foam latte from somewhere else.

The Storyville experience strips coffee down to its essence: ground beans and water. Yet its coffee is more than just great quality coffee beans. There is a ritual associated with making the perfect cup that includes every small detail. You can see it in the tutorial videos offered on the Storyville site, as well as the story of the company's custom-designed coffee mug, which it commissioned after an unsatisfying search for the perfect coffee mug led them to design it themselves. What Storyville Coffee is really selling is what it calls the ultimate coffee experience.

What do Storyville Coffee and Moo.com have in common? They both have built their brands on the passion of their founders and employees for what they are selling. In the process, they have each created a unique backstory their customers can believe in.

GO TO GUIDE p.261

Inspired Inventor Story: Innovation That Really Sucks

When David Oreck, founder of the $100 million Oreck Corporation, was asked about his decision to name his vacuum cleaner business after himself, he responded by saying, "I felt there was a facelessness and namelessness to this business, and I felt that I would have an advantage if people knew who they were doing business with."[4] Ironically, today the vacuum cleaner brand best known for succeeding based on the personality of the founder is not Oreck, but a company founded much later than Oreck by a man who spent the early 1970s selling crazy inventions like the "sea truck" (a cross between a pickup truck and a whaler) and the

[4] www.industryweek.com/ReadArticle.aspx?ArticleID=10058

"ballbarrow" (a wheelbarrow that used an easy to maneuver ball instead of a wheel).

That inventor's name is James Dyson and in the late 1980s he found his true calling by setting out to create the perfect vacuum cleaner that would not lose suction. The process took more than five years and more than 5,000 prototypes, but in 1986, in Japan, Dyson released his very first bagless suction vacuum cleaner, called the "G Force." It cost $2,000 and became an instant status symbol in Japan.

Dyson's original intention was to sell the technology to an existing manufacturer, but no one was willing to cannibalize their revenue from replacement bags with Dyson's bagless concept. So after his hit in Japan, he used the funds from that success to finance the development of a model for the United States. He patented as his "Root Cyclone" technology and defended it vigorously (he sued Hoover in a UK court for copying his design, and won).

The bagless vacuum itself was a powerful idea, but it did not find a truly passionate following until Dyson released a series of television and print ads featuring himself talking honestly about how hard he had worked to create the perfect vacuum cleaner and pledged that "nothing gets clogged, ever." He was believable, likeable, and offered an authentic story that consumers responded to. He was the ultimate inspired inventor.

Today, customers rave about their Dyson vacuums online (just take a look at any of the hundreds of positive reviews on Amazon.com) and credit Dyson himself with forging a bond with his customers. Some women thanked him for creating a product that made the men in their lives want to clean. Others talked about the pride they take in their vacuums and how they cannot help talking to others about the vacuum cleaner. The brand itself stands for innovation, even going so far as to offer advice on their corporate Web site for aspiring inventors about how to patent their inventions and sell them. Dyson himself published his own autobiography in 2003, about innovation, invention, and the secrets behind the Dyson patented model. He called it *Against the Odds.*

Inspired Inventor Story: The Secret of the Best Restaurant in the World

When we talk about invention, we are usually referring to a new product or technology, as in Dyson's case. Invention can come in different forms, though, especially when it comes from mixing two disciplines that usually have little to do with one another. One of the most interesting examples of this is a type of cuisine inspired by physics and chemistry that takes center stage at what *Restaurant* magazine has rated the Best Restaurant in the World for the past two years running.

The restaurant is El Bulli, an uncommon destination located off a winding mountain road in Roses on the Costa Brava about two hours north of Barcelona. The head chef, Ferran Adrià, began his career as a dishwasher and now travels six months out of the year (during which time the restaurant is closed) developing his trademark 30-course tasting menu. He was recently named by *Time* magazine as one of the most innovative thinkers of the twenty-first century.

What makes El Bulli—despite its being closed six months out of the year to allow the chefs to travel and redefine the menu—the best in the world? The answer is a technique pioneered by Adrià called *molecular gastronomy,* which helps him and his team of top chefs create food that seems inspired by science fiction to those who sample it. Adrià dislikes the term molecular gastronomy, instead referring to his creations as "deconstructionist" for how they break down flavors independently. His techniques include creating something called "culinary foam," which is described as taking natural flavors, mixing them with a gelling agent such as agar, and putting them through a whipped cream canister equipped with N_2O cartridges. If it sounds complicated, it should. Only a handful of restaurants in the world use this method.

One of them belongs to José Andrés, a former disciple in Adrià's kitchen, and now a winner of the prestigious James Beard Foundation Award and owner of a range of restaurants in Washington, D.C. One of his restaurants is the iconic "minibar," often spoken of by locals (including me) as the most unique dining experience in D.C. The restaurant offers its own 30-course molecular gastronomy tasting menu in a small bar that seats just eight tucked upstairs at the back of Café Atlantico restaurant in downtown Washington. The entire experience of being presented with each dish as the team of four chefs behind the counter prepare it and describe it for you is one of a kind. You simply cannot dine at minibar without telling people about it.

Chef Wylie Dufresne's WD-50 restaurant on the Lower East Side in Manhattan offers a similarly talkable experience. Chef Wylie was even a finalist on the popular television show *Iron Chef* in 2006. At WD-50, guests with a party 14 can schedule a private dining session in the kitchen with Wylie himself as your guide through the meal. In May 2006, *Fast Company* magazine also ran a cover story on this new science of cuisine, featuring a chef named Homaru Cantu and calling him "Edison of the Edible." Cantu's Moto restaurant in Chicago is regularly on the list of hottest up and coming restaurants and his mission, as he described it in the *Fast Company* piece, is to "change the way humans perceive food."[5]

Clearly the idea of molecular gastronomy captures the imagination of foodies and travelers everywhere. It may be the most innovative new trend in cuisine of the past 50 years. Just about every restaurant ever

[5] http://www.fastcompany.com/magazine/105/open_food-cantu.html

opened is the result of someone somewhere who is passionate about food. What each of these inspired chefs have managed to do is tell a story of invention that makes their restaurants more than just places to eat. They are now destinations.

Similarly, Dyson has made his story central to how he sells his product. What all of these scientific chefs and James Dyson were able to do was think differently about their business or industry and use their inspiration and enthusiasm to create something new. Regardless of the culture, people respond to inventors and innovations. They create wonderful things, and we can't help sharing their stories with others.

GO TO GUIDE p.262

Smart Listener Story: Google's Art of Failing Wisely

Smart listening is not about focus groups, pilot programs, or other formalized ways to test ideas. Those all have their place, but the idea of smart listening is something more fundamental. Insight may come from these scripted efforts, but listening is not the same as product or prototype testing. The stories of smart listeners are the ones about organizations that are listening to their customers in order to understand their needs and the *gaps* that they can fill with a product or service. The companies that fit the story model for smart listeners are the ones that create their business or products based on listening to what people want.

Google does this extremely well. Perhaps more than any other company, Google has embraced a policy of listening to people, putting an idea out there and letting individuals play with it, and then using the early feedback to improve it. In October 2007, Matt Glotzbach, product management director for Google Enterprise gave a keynote speech at the Interop IT Conference and Exposition in New York. During the speech, he shared that a core part of Google's strategy when launching new products was to "fail wisely" and that the practice of sitting on a new product for years while testing was outdated.

Anyone who has followed Google's approach to launching new products knows that the way the company approaches this is very focused on user feedback, but not in a closed way. Open beta versions of new products are launched almost every week. Those ideas that work are further revised, and those that don't are quickly abandoned. If smart listening involves fast response to what customers are saying, then Google has one of the best models in the world to capture relevant feedback and act on it. This approach is a key part of their backstory and what makes their brand one that people routinely rate as one of the most innovative in the world.

Smart Listener Story: Stacy's Sidewalk Pita Cart

Another smart listener who used customer feedback to launch her own successful business in a slightly different way was Stacy Madison. When Stacy first decided to leave her career in social work and follow her dream of entering the food business, she did it by buying a sidewalk cart serving all-natural pita sandwiches on the street in downtown Boston with her business partner, Mark Andrus. The idea of a social worker reinventing her life to try something new is a character story most people can relate to.

At the original Stacy's D'lites cart, the sandwiches were so popular that she soon had lines around the block. To keep the customers happily waiting, she decided to bake pita chips and hand them out to people as they waited in line. After some time spent watching her customers and listening to their pleas for her to start selling these chips, she starting doing exactly that and Stacy's Pita Chips was born.

As with many regional products like this, people loved the product but it was only likely to travel so far. In early 2007, the company decided to focus on creating a buzz through word of mouth by taking its backstory and retelling it to a new audience across America. The idea was to send boxes of pita chips to more than 100,000 people named "Stacy" so they could build a group of enthusiasts and introduce new people to the product based on the uniting factor that they all had the same first name. The campaign worked, generating a huge buzz online: photos were posted on blogs from Stacys who received the mailing; hundreds of e-mails with positive feedback turned up in Stacy's inbox, and the brand attracted many new customers.

Although Google and Stacy's Pita Chips have taken slightly different approaches to how they listen to their customers, each has the concept of "smart listening" at the heart of the growth of its business.

GO TO GUIDE p. 264

Likeable Hero Story: Microlending to Change Lives

Premal Shah is a good example of a likeable hero; he is the soft-spoken president of Kiva.org—a Web site that is changing the world through its pioneering approach to microfinance. Meeting him is like meeting a brilliant but obsessed inventor who is always considering new ways to improve his inventions. For Premal, the obsession is finding more ways to make Kiva.org more efficient in its mission of lending money in "microloan" amounts to entrepreneurs in third world countries.

Microfinance and microlending are the Nobel Prize–winning concepts from Muhammad Yunus that introduced the idea of offering small "micro" loans of tens or hundreds of dollars to empower third world entrepreneurs. Kiva.org, along with Yunus's own Grameen Bank, are two leading organizations in this field, offering up millions of dollars in loans each year. The real power of Kiva.org, however, is that it is a platform for you as an individual to loan a certain amount of money directly to an entrepreneur. This was never before possible.

The old model of aid where large international organizations throw billions of dollars toward large projects while corrupt governments siphon off large percentages of the aid no longer works. That model has come under considerable criticism recently through talks by leading thinkers at influential events like the Technology Entertainment Design (TED) conference and World Economic Forum, books like *Globalization and Its Discontents* by Joseph E. Stiglitz (another Nobel Prize winner). Fighting corruption is a major priority now at some of the top international banking institutions, including the International Monetary Fund (IMF), Asian Development Bank, and World Bank.[6]

Smarter solutions that empower people are needed. Kiva.org is one of the sites that offers solutions like this—and is based on a powerful insight. When you loan money to Kiva, the first thing you realize is that it is a loan and not a donation. The power of this idea is vast. You are not offering charity to someone; you are giving them a chance to make an idea they have into a reality. The most interesting thing about this model is the importance of repayment.

The reason this is so significant is that it allows recipients of help to keep the one thing that is so often taken away from them: pride. When someone is able to pay you back for funds that you helped them with, their pride is intact. Accepting charity means swallowing your pride and doing what you need to do because you have no alternative. Offering people pride leads to empowerment and empowerment leads to real change. The story of Kiva.org is one of offering empowerment and what the site realizes is that this is the one thing that people in developing countries need above all else.

---

[6] My father, a longtime leader at the World Bank, even wrote a book on this called *Challenging Corruption in Asia*.

The site itself is a collection of backstories from people who are in need of funds to make their ideas happen. Browsing these real stories is a humbling experience, as you learn firsthand just how much someone halfway across the world could do with just a few hundred dollars. It is enough to make you consider returning your brand-new Dyson vacuum cleaner in favor of putting the money toward a more noble use.

The power of the Kiva.org story is not just in the idea or the technology, but in the story of the founding and the team members, from Premal to others, who decided to do something to change the world. Everyone who lends money through Kiva.org knows this backstory, and it is a key part of why they choose to support the site.

Likeable Hero Story: A Pastor with Personality

In case you haven't noticed, religion has a pretty severe branding problem. From Jehovah's Witnesses knocking on doors trying to convert people, to the violence across the world inflicted by people of one faith on those of another in the name of religion—most religions come with some sort of bias from those who believe, or those who refute it. Yet all these polarized opinions when it comes to religion are often the result of ignorance or a lack of personal interaction with individuals who could bring those religions to life.

Religion is as much about faith as it is about the people that you associate with, whether they are the leaders of a religion or your fellow believers. It may sound crass to look at it in this sense, but faith needs personality just as much as any business does.

One blogger who knows this well is a San Francisco native named Bruce Reyes-Chow. His blog is an exploration of spirituality and faith and could fit well into any list of religiously oriented blogs (of which there are thousands). Bruce, however, is also an ordained Presbyterian minister and leads a congregation at the Mission Bay Community Church (MBCC). His blog is all about his weekly sermons, and his self-described life as a "pastor, geek, dad, and follower of Christ." Blogging may seem like an odd thing for a pastor to do religiously (pun intended), but what is even more unique about Bruce's blog is just how openly he shares his thoughts and ideas.

Once, after a particularly tough Sunday sermon, Bruce called his own sermon a "one way ticket to sucksville" and apologized for confusing his churchgoers and promised to do better the following week. This is not the kind of relationship most people expect to have with a preacher. Bruce is real, engaging, open and honest, and the community responds on his blog with loyalty and words of encouragement for his rare moments of confusion. The blog is a core part of the experience at MBCC. Bruce himself notes that the blog "allows folks to get to know a little bit more about me before taking the risk of coming to church on Sunday. . .and about 75% of the people who visit our church have read my blog before ever setting foot in our church."

To understand how unique this experience is, let's look at a national institution in the Philippines called the "Iglesia Ni Cristo," ironically bearing the acronym INC. The name (loosely translated) means "Church of Christ," translated into Tagalog and across the Philippines you will hardly be able to go to any city without spotting dozens of Iglesia Ni Cristo churches spread out across the city, which are located as strategically as one might find fast food restaurants in America. One look at the ubiquitous yellow-topped chain of churches and you could be forgiven for thinking that these help take religion to a new level of standardization. Bruce's vision for the MBCC is a clear contrast, and offers his congregation a far different experience. Along the way, Bruce offers a backstory that is easy to become engaged with, no matter what your religion.

GO TO GUIDE p.266

Little Guy versus Big Guy Story: Taking on the Biggest Brand in the World

Back in 1996, Kevin Plank was promoting his new brand of athletic sportswear called Under Armour by doing exactly what his biggest competitor did more than 30 years earlier. Driving his Ford Explorer to college football games, he sold his unique brand of apparel to college football athletes, including many of his own former teammates at the University of Maryland. Ironically reminiscent of how Phil Knight once sold sneakers to runners from the trunk of his car to start Nike, Plank realized early that the best endorsement for his products was to get athletes to wear them and tell others about it.

His challenge was huge—to take on the firmly entrenched sports apparel leaders in Nike and Adidas in an industry that many thought would be impenetrable. To do it, he used word-of-mouth marketing and sampling. As a former college athlete, he had many relationships with universities in his local area and started by supplying players at his former team at the University of Maryland with his distinctive undershirts, which he sold under the brand Under Armour.

His vision came from a dual understanding of what he had to sell. The first and most logical product benefit was a brand of underwear that was specifically designed to be worn under football pads, not absorb sweat like cotton did, and dry much faster. The second element was far more important. His line of shirts were tight and bore a distinctive logo on the chest, making the wearers part of a club. This was not the typical Nike swoosh that every athlete knew. Plank had something different and it began to mean something to the athletes who wore it. This was an entirely new category of performance apparel.

The conflict in this story, of course, is that Nike and Adidas and Reebok and all the other sports companies making apparel saw the trend

Under Armour started and moved quickly to take advantage of it. In the years since Under Armour has taken off, each of the big competitors has launched its own line of ultradry, moisture-repelling fabrics designed for exactly the same uses as Under Armour. Under Armour was the little guy taking on all the big guys, but still has managed to win because it has been able to tell a convincing backstory that engages consumers and builds a relationship with loyal customers.

The company's triumph comes not only from having existed for more than 10 years and continued to grow its business, but for its willingness to take on Nike and its other largest competitors head-on. The underlying message in this story is that this is a brand not afraid to fight. In 2006, UA even launched its own brand of footwear, moving beyond apparel. Clearly, people love an underdog.

Little Guy versus Big Guy Story—Bugaboo Strollers and Hip Moms

It may seem like there is an inverse relationship between being a parent and having style. Though becoming a parent may have something to do with it, a more likely culprit is that most products for new parents are just not that fashionable. The leader by all accounts in the baby product industry is one whose Web site describes it as focused on "product safety, quality, reliability and convenience." Style or fashion are not high on the list. Yet this company, called Graco, has been around for more than 60 years making cribs, strollers, car seats, highchairs, swings, bouncers, activity centers, and just about any other baby-related product you can imagine. Along the way, the company developed several product innovations, including the baby swing and the now-common car seat travel system that allows you to take out a car seat with young babies in it while leaving the base in the car.

Taking on the dominance of Graco in the baby products industry seems like it would be an impossible feat, particularly when the company is so singularly focused on the one element that they believe is most important to parents—safety. As it turns out, there is another concern for many urban new parents that had been going unfulfilled. That need was perfectly illustrated by the character Miranda on the popular show *Sex in the City* in 2002. Despite her new status as a parent, her life still revolved around being an urban professional in Manhattan, which meant she was not ready to abandon all fashion and enter the bonds of styleless parenthood. As part of her rebellion, she pushed around the streets of Manhattan a new stroller that few had ever seen before that program aired.

The stroller was called the Frog, made by a Dutch company with a funny name: Bugaboo. This Bugaboo stroller looked like a cross between an art piece and a pushcart. It also looked unlike any other stroller on the market, and made an obvious statement for any parent pushing it down the street. The stroller was an instant hit, becoming the ultimate symbol of urban cool for city-dwelling parents in cities around the world. Many parents describe it as the major "splurge" in their baby-related purchases, and it certainly qualifies with most models retailing for more than $500 (and some well over the $1,000 mark).

Despite its superpremium positioning, Bugaboo started as a small challenger brand in Holland, never intending to take on the world's largest baby products maker or become the company behind *the* must-have product for upwardly mobile new parents everywhere. The company began as a partnership between designer Max Barenbrug and his brother-in-law, physician Eduard Zanen. The original goal was to sell the idea of the stroller to one of the big guys. After trying unsuccessfully to find a buyer, Barenbrug decided to commission it himself by "opening the yellow pages for Taipei and looking under stroller manufacturers" as the Bugaboo Web site describes only partly in jest. As Barenbrug noted in an interview several years after the Bugaboo arrived in the United States, "Most companies are too focused on the products of other companies. . .they focus on a cost rather than a vision."[7]

At Bugaboo, unlike many other small companies, its heritage is not dominated by the founders, but by the many people who work at the company headquarters in Holland and share its passion. The company's corporate philosophy stresses being different, and team members are encouraged to share their opinions and take responsibility for their roles and actions. While most other stroller makers focus their marketing on features, safety ratings, or how washable their covers are, Bugaboo focuses its marketing on the lifestyle and freedom that its strollers can provide for "adventure-seeking parents."

The product marketing has lived up to this positioning, with smart efforts such as a series of 22 commissioned artist-produced downloadable maps with kid-friendly walking tours in cities around the globe called "Bugaboo Daytrips," as well as a wonderfully creative Broadway dance show–style film created by their ad agency, 72andSunny, to introduce the new lightweight Bugaboo Bee stroller. The video and Daytrips sites were both viral hits, getting sent around from parent to parent and both managing to do the one thing that few baby products manage to effectively do—target fathers as well as mothers.

Even their product launch strategy abandons the big chain stores in favor of working with small independent baby stores like Genius Jones in Miami, a store which focuses on carrying baby products that are well-designed. As further example of its status appeal, Bugaboo strollers are now the product of choice for celebrity moms to wheel their tots around

---

[7] http://www.businessweek.com/innovate/content/aug2005/id20050831_266835.htm

in, including Madonna, Gwyneth Paltrow, Sarah Jessica Parker, and a growing list of other stars.

Seeing the strollers on the street inspires other parents or potential parents to look at those strollers with envy. The backstory Bugaboo managed to tell was one of passionate European designers who set out to add an element of style to the decidedly unstylish life of a parent. This story perfectly matched the ones their customers wanted to tell about themselves. Parents who pushed a Bugaboo stroller around town were still hip and cool, despite being parents. Most important, it gave regular parents the chance to believe they were part of an elite group by having the most luxurious stroller you could buy, just like the celebrities.

GO TO GUIDE p.267

What ties all these stories together? They all follow the BArc Model, but even more important, they offer a reason to believe. Storyville Coffee customers subscribe because they believe that coffee expires and that

A Reason to Believe

the market for something to believe in is infinite

(c)gapingvoid.com

a quality cup of coffee is worth some effort. Athletes who wear Under Armour do so because of the feature benefits of the clothing, but also because they believe in the story behind the company that was built by athletes for athletes. A marketing backstory gives your customers a reason to believe in your brand.

One thing you may have noticed about these stories is that they offer many overlaps. Dyson may have been an inspired inventor, but he was also a little guy versus a big buy. Google is a smart listener as well as an inspired inventor. The idea of these models of backstories is not that they must be mutually exclusive. It is always possible for a company's story to take on aspects of any story. The point is that there is one story that offers the best description of what defines your organization. The real trick is to understand which one this is and to develop your backstory from there.

The theme that each of these stories shares is the focus on the people behind the products or services that are the purpose for the company's existence. Backstories are a way of bringing out the human story behind your brand. This is not a product development story or "company history" in the strictest sense of how a company moves. Think of it less as a company history and more as a family history. Family histories are highly personal and involve people who bring each generation to life.

Creating a backstory requires a different way of thinking about the foundation of your organization, but is not likely to cause any serious resistance within your company. The reason is that you are usually just changing the way that the story behind your company is described. This is the basis of personality, but it is where you go from here that will require the most significant change in your communications. From now on, this is where you will likely find the most roadblocks—I'll focus on how to contend with the roadblocks in Chapter 5. Once we discuss how to navigate these roadblocks, you'll be ready to really start using your personality for marketing.

The Sellevator Pitch

4

A backstory offers a reason for your customers to believe in your brand. There are five key models of backstories: the passionate enthusiast, the inspired inventor, the smart listener, the likeable hero, and the little guy versus the big guy.

Chapter 5

Conquering the Fear Factor

Getting Your Organization to Embrace Personality

Heather Armstrong has a few words of caution for anyone who has considered blogging about work: "Be Ye Not So Stupid." She writes the popular blog Dooce. What happened to her in 2002 gave rise to the commonly accepted term of "getting Dooced," which according to Wikipedia (today) means "to lose one's job as a result of something one wrote on the Internet." As Heather describes her situation on her Web site:

> I started this website in February 2001. A year later I was fired from my job for this website because I had written stories that included people in my workplace. My advice to you is BE YE NOT SO STUPID. Never write about work on the internet unless your boss knows and sanctions the fact that YOU ARE WRITING ABOUT WORK ON THE INTERNET.

Luckily, the ending is happy for Heather, who has since joined the Federated Media network of superstar bloggers and now makes enough

money from the advertising on her blog to support her family. But her story illustrates one of the more visible dangers of focusing on personality at work (and, specifically, with starting a blog).

In her case, it was her own personality exhibited through a blog that got her into trouble. For others, becoming an accidental spokesperson may create this moment of danger, or it may come from advocating a new way of thinking within a company. Whatever the trigger, one of the first fears you will likely need to overcome if you are going to champion using personality within your organization is the fear of getting fired.

Finding Your Authority

Getting fired is surely not a fear for everyone, right? In time, you may either reach a point where you are indispensable to a company, or even

own your own company. What is it about people in those roles
them to avoid the fear of losing their jobs? For those who have their
own company, the answer is simple. They control their organization and,
for better or worse, also control their own destiny. That is likely one reason they started their own business in the first place.

Yet even business owners can find themselves in a vulnerable position, not because of fear of losing their job, but for fear of losing something far more important—their authority. This is where the lesson is
universal. If you want to lead a change within your organization, you
have to do it from a point of authority. This does not mean you need to
be the boss or even at a top level of an organization. Authority, to some
degree, is like respect—you only get it if you earn it. We all know that
position titles do not equate with respect in most cases. Respect derives
from performance, not a title on a business card.

The way to earn it (or avoid losing it) is to focus on one simple
word: buy-in. Okay, maybe that's two words. Either way, buy-in means
that people believe that what you are doing is correct and support you.
They are ready to follow you, and do what you think you need to do
because you have convinced them it is the right way to go.

You may have noticed that this is quite similar to a common definition of leadership, which is the ability to inspire people to follow you even
if they do not know where you are going. Trust, respect, and belief are
all elements that factor into this. When you have true authority, you have
all of these elements as well.

GO TO GUIDE p. 271 Establishing your authority within an organization is the
first step toward helping your company to better demonstrate
its own personality. You need to do this in order to become
credible (authority precedes credibility). See the guide in Part Two to learn
how you can establish your authority.

Why Personality Makes Some Organizations Nervous

Once you have started to establish a basis of credibility within your company, the next step is usually tackling the roadblocks. Before you do, it is important to understand why personality seems like such a risky idea for some organizations. We have already referred to several reasons for this throughout the first four chapters:

1. It requires you to embrace your accidental spokespeople.
2. It involves sharing control with your customers.
3. It takes more work than using brainless policies and standard "corporate language."
4. It forces you to be more open, honest, and transparent about what you do.

I have intentionally postponed discussing these issues in detail because the bulk of the book so far has focused on presenting you with the argument for why your organization needs a personality and how to understand what it is and how to start to recognize and foster it. It is now time to talk about those things that may hinder you. Whether you are an employee trying to start an uphill surge toward reinventing the way your company communicates or you have your own small business and want to promote it more aggressively, this chapter will help you get past the things that may stand in your way.

Fear and Beyond

When you look at the list of reasons why personality makes brands nervous, you will notice that underlying all of those reasons is a single emotion—fear. Fear as a factor in holding companies back from thinking differently and/or from innovating has been the topic of many recent books. Fear, however, is too broad a subject to treat as one universal emotion or as the universal cause of all obstacles to embracing personality. And for me to tell you simply to find a way to help your organization conquer its fear is too simplistic a solution—because fear in our culture is "macro." It is all around us, like water; we live in a culture in which so much of the media we see, hear, and read is infused with fear-driven messages that it has become expected.

Fear is the basis for almost all of the stories we read in our newspapers and magazines, the dramas and sitcoms we watch on TV or at the movies, and in many places on the Internet too. Terror alerts around the world flash in alarming colors like orange and red at moments when we are powerless to do anything about them. Advertisements everywhere continually proclaim the dangers of being too fat, too skinny, too old, etc. Don't make a mistake or get swindled; instead, log on to www.wetellyouthetruth.com and avoid the scammers. Don't get sued, buy legal coverage. Oh, and don't forget to tune into your local news to learn what you don't know about your shoelaces that could kill you.

The list of fear-inspired messages is nearly endless. As author Bernard Goldberg noted in his book *Bias: A CBS Insider Exposes How the Media Distort the News*, "Scaring the hell out of people makes for good TV, even when it makes for shallow journalism." It is the dark side of media and a common trick in a world where news has become entertainment and substance is overtaken by shock or awe.

The reason I bring up this culture of fear is that the net effect of this media is that we as individuals tend to build a cautious view of the world, a cautious view also makes businesses reluctant to try a new model of communications or to share too much information authentically about itself or its employees.

A culture built on fear leads to individuals and companies that are afraid of change. This is a fear I have seen firsthand in colleagues and clients unwilling to take a risk, stuck on following conventions, blindly

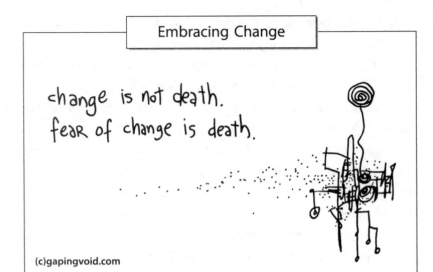

change is not death.
fear of change is death.

(c)gapingvoid.com

taking orders, and never doing anything remarkable. I'm betting you've seen it too.

Induhviduals Fear Change

None of us want to be in an organization like that the one referred to in the cartoon above, yet many businesses unwittingly encourage their workplaces to become exactly like this. We have already discussed some of the ways this happens, such as the employee-silencing policy we learned about in Chapter 1. These choices lead to an organization filled with automatons who follow rules and wait for the bell to ring to be done for the day. They are the *in"duh"viduals* that Scott Adams, the creator of the *Dilbert* comic strip, frequently pokes fun at. They are the monkeys that CareerBuilder.com featured in its series of highly popular television ads that bring to life the feeling we have all had at one point in our working lives of being stuck working with less evolved colleagues.

We already know you're no induhvidual, though, because you have your knuckles firmly off the ground and are holding this book right now (a fact that already puts you one rung higher than your colleagues on the evolutionary ladder). So, this section is for you, the one who has come this far toward realizing the promise of how personality can help your organization and now need a method to help you get past the naysayers and conquer the fear of change within your team or among your customers.

Whether you are in the middle of a huge and seemingly unmovable enterprise, or the head of the business, you are still likely to find barriers.

GO TO GUIDE *p.* **274** As we have already discussed, fear is the underlying emotion, but to do something about it, you need to understand where the fear is coming from. In most organizations, the fear originates in one of four key places: success, uncertainty, tradition, or precedent.

Four Great Barriers to Personality

1. Success—What we are doing is already working.
2. Uncertainty—We don't know what will happen.
3. Tradition—We have always done it this way.
4. Precedent—No one else is doing it that way.

These are the four great barriers to a company's developing its own personality, and throughout the rest of this chapter we will explore the ways that you can spot which one of these barriers exists within your organization, and then try to find a way to overcome it. Let's start with what many of you are likely to consider the most surprising barrier—success.

The Danger of Success

If what you are doing is already working, and you are selling your product to a satisfied customer, the obvious question is: why change? Being currently successful is the first great barrier to personality, because it is easy to have the impression that everything is fine. This is a dangerous thought, because it leads to many undesirable results, like arrogance, complacency, and a loss of ambition. Many of the companies that fail are the ones that were winners but could not see the next threat coming and ultimately were overtaken by competitors.

Netscape was the leading Internet browser until it was overtaken by Microsoft's Internet Explorer. Polaroid ruled instant printing, until digital photography took off and people stopped printing photos. The world is full of examples of companies that have been successful at what they do and enjoyed a profitable existence, until something happened and they were left in the dust.

The unfortunate cliché that epitomizes this false perception of success as a lasting situation is the saying, "if it ain't broke, don't fix it." The problem with this view is that we often use the wrong tools to figure out if it's broken. Consider these truths:

1. Making money doing something today is no indication that you will be able to make money doing the same thing tomorrow.
2. Having a satisfied customer does not mean you will hold on to that customer when competitors come along.

Do you still believe that you can hold on to your customers doing the same thing you have always done, or that only broken things need fixing? The barrier of success just doesn't hold up when you look at the history of companies that have for too long coasted on past glory and have counted on it lasting. Having a successful and profitable company means this is the perfect time to embrace a change that can help you connect more deeply with your customers. Not doing so can mean the difference between keeping your success and watching it fade as a competitor takes your place. To explore this further in an example, let's turn our lens to the world of comic books.

Manga and the Death of Superman

In 1993, DC Comics killed Superman. Actually, a character named Doomsday did it, but with sales of comic books sagging and consumer interest steadily shrinking, DC Comics needed a big stunt to revive interest and the death of Superman was it. Killing off their most successful comic superhero and a worldwide icon generated huge international press. People knew it was coming and lined up outside of comic book stores to get the comics in a way they had not done for years. The death of Superman was great for the comic book business, for a short time.

One person who cautioned DC Comics against this ill-advised move was comic enthusiast Chuck Rozanski, owner of a chain of comic book shops in Colorado called Mile High Comics. He writes an insightful weekly column online about the comic book industry called "Tales from the Database." In one of those columns he wrote about "The Death of Superman," and shared what really happened and why that moment may have been the beginning of the end of the comic book industry as it once was.

> People who had little, if any, previous interest in comics mobbed stores on the day that SUPERMAN #75 was released, some standing in line for hours to purchase just a single copy. . . . There was only one problem with this entire program. It was based entirely on a lie.

DC never had any intention of actually killing off Superman. His entire "death" was an event solely contrived to sell lots and lots of comic books. . . . When these new comics consumers/investors tried to sell their copies of SUPERMAN #75 for a profit a few months later, however, and discovered that they could only recover their purchase price if they had a first printing, their bitter disillusionment did much to cause the comics investing bubble to begin bursting

With over a decade behind us now since that ill-advised promotion was first conceptualized, I believe that all of us in the world of comics are still paying the price for the "death" of Superman . . . I continue to hear from at least one non-comics fan a month about how they felt ripped off when they were "tricked" into believing that Superman was really going to die. By the end of 1993, it became painfully clear to anyone who studied the market numbers that the comics world was starting to shrink. Little did we know, however, that the decline would last for more than a decade, and would eventually reduce the overall unit sales volume of comics by a disastrous 80% from the 1992 peak.

Corresponding to this loss in sales volume was an evolution of comic culture over the past half century that Douglas Wolk described in his 2007 book *Reading Comics: How Graphic Novels Work and What They Mean* as "an insular, self-feeding, self-loathing, self-defeating fly-trap."[1] Recently, this comic culture has started to find a new hero (so to speak) in Manga, a new genre and style of graphic novel that originated in Japan. The worldwide hit television show *Heroes* has a story format loosely based on the serialized style of these graphic novels. Manga has already grown to a more than $200-million-per-year business in the United States, and is similarly popular worldwide.

[1] *Reading Comics: How Graphic Novels Work and What They Mean* (Wolk), p. 64.

In the November 2007 issue of *Wired* magazine, the cover story was titled "Manga Conquers America," and inside writer Daniel H. Pink reported extensively about how Manga was redefining the comic book world and making DC Comics (and its longtime rival Marvel) less relevant.

How could *Spiderman*, *Superman*, and *Batman* get displaced by these serialized black-and-white graphic novels from the other side of the world? They were beloved icons, around since World War II, and there is certainly no shortage of Hollywood support for these franchises, as the film industry churns out sequel after sequel of these reliable superhero movies. The reason comes down to a simple difference in the premise behind each story that is reflected in the majority of Manga as well as in the creation of *Heroes*.

Manga features real people in crazy situations in a serialized story-line format using a storyboard style. DC Comics and Marvel strips are in a very standard panel style. Manga uses a more flowing design where the story unfolds in an artistic way, but not necessarily in neat little rectangular boxes. What is interesting is that most American superheroes were, for the most part, just born or accidentally became superheroes (through some freak radioactive accident or spiderbite). The heroes in most Manga-style comics evolve from real people facing extraordinary circumstances. Manga is seldom about "superpowers," but more about ordinary everyday people evolving while in heroic situations.

Manga is real, engaging, and involves more than just your usual comic readers (the stated audience that reads Manga in the United States is nearly 60 percent female, as opposed to a heavy male skew for "traditional" American comics). Marvel and DC Comics have good franchises and still enjoy some success, but all signs point to the real growth in the comic industry coming from Manga . . . and that means that no matter how powerful they once were, the legendary superheroes of the past may still be left behind.

₋₋ story of what happened to the comic book industry demonstrates that there is no such thing as infinite success. What is working today should give you the license to try something new while you are still on top. As John F. Kennedy famously said, "the best time to fix the roof is when the sun is shining." If you need to innovate after you have been replaced, you are already too late.

The key to overcoming the success barrier is debunking the idea that it "ain't broke." Actually, it *is* broken. . .because you are not thinking about the next threat around the corner.

Monsters in the Closet

The second great barrier to a company developing its own personality is the uncertainty factor. When you feel that you don't know what to expect or are in an unfamiliar situation, then you can become paralyzed and unable to conquer your fear. The classic example of this is being afraid of the monsters in the closet when you were a kid. You might know subconsciously that it's not a reasonable suspicion and that the monsters are not really in there, but you can't help thinking about it because it's dark and you just can't see inside that closet to be sure. Not knowing makes it scary.

The only way to get past this fear is to reframe the question you are accustomed to asking. Do not ask what will happen if you go to sleep—ask what will happen if you *don't* check the closet to see if the monsters are actually there. In business, if you don't add personality to the way you communicate with your customers, you will continue to be faceless, your customers will seek a more authentic relationship, and it will be only a matter of time before they find it from one of your competitors. The secret is to turn from thinking about the consequences of *action* to the consequences of *inaction*.

Once you do this, the benefits of changing become apparent. Everyone's favorite current example of a company that has done this is Dell. Dell is the overused example of what used to be a faceless company not listening to its customers and getting criticized through social media. Blogger Jeff Jarvis started the storm in 2005 when his series of blog post complaints about Dell's poor customer service led to "Dell hell" in 2005, in which a storm of customer complaints surfaced online and Dell refused to answer or engage them.

The Real Secret of Dell's Success

It wasn't too long before Dell took Jarvis's advice and started reading and writing blogs and joined in the conversation. Indeed, it has actively begun listening and reaching out to bloggers, and the company has overhauled its customer service process, cut the number of outsourcing partners, and changed the metric by which these teams are measured (from speed to resolutions). It has created its own blog called Direct2Dell, where lead blogger Lionel Menchaca openly responds to customer frustrations and puts a real face on Dell.

Dell even brought back Michael Dell himself to run the company, and in February 2007 he launched a site dedicated to online collaboration with Dell's customers called IdeaStorm that led to ideas for real products. Dell crawled out of the hole it had put itself in, a point that was most visibly made in October 2007 when *BusinessWeek* published an article with the headline "Dell Learns to Listen." The piece offered the conclusion that Dell had gone from "worst to first," and, most significant, it was written by Jeff Jarvis himself.

As Dell showed, conquering its own monsters and reinventing the way it communicated with customers was ultimately the best way to bring the company up out of "hell" and back to a position of leadership in the tech industry. The real secret that led to Dell's renewed credibility, however, is not the passion or conviction of one star blogger. It is the company's engagement in the dialogue on a consistent basis. Today when there is a blog post talking about Dell products, very often there will be a Dell employee who is commenting and sharing the company's real point of view from a real person. Dell has managed to conquer and overturn its own employee-silencing policy, for the better of the company. The message the company now sends loud and clear is that it is listening and that it cares. When someone from Dell comments on the blog, that person does not fear receiving a negative comment in return; she or he is expecting to start a conversation and knows that that is not what will occur. This is how knowledge can conquer uncertainty.

Conquering the Uncertainty Barrier

GO TO
GUIDE
p.278

Uncertainty is all about a lack of knowledge. When you have no idea how your actions may be interpreted, then you will naturally be more reluctant to try something new. In part, this is the reason that GPS works so well, as Ogilvy & Mather's Vice Chairman Rory Sutherland so eloquently summed up in his opening remarks at the annual Ogilvy Verge event in London in 2007. The GPS makes experimentation acceptable because the cost of making a mistake is low. You can be right back on course very quickly. Part of conquering uncertainty is finding a way to demonstrate that mistakes or mishaps will not take you too far off course. The other part is collecting knowledge to counter the uncertainty.

Stick to the Status Quo

To understand the third barrier, let's go back to early 2006, when the Disney Channel aired an original movie that was supposed to get only a few hundred thousand viewers, if that. The telefilm, called *High School*

Musical, was a modern-day adaptation of *Romeo and Juliet* in which high school kids would break out into song at random times true to the standard format of most musicals. The show became a surprise hit, with more than 7 million viewers tuning in to its premiere broadcast, and inspired a concert tour, stage musical, ice show, book, and a sequel film in 2007.

One of the most popular songs from the show features high school students admitting that they love to do things that are completely out of character for their "types." A basketball player wants to be a baker, a chubby bookworm wants to be a hip-hop dancer, and around them all the other students are telling them to "stick to the status quo" (through song and dance, of course). It is a reflection of what most of us remember high school to be. . .a struggle to do what is expected and fit in.

Unfortunately, there are many workplaces that are still like that, where the pressure to stick to the status quo pervades everything you try to do. Often, the status quo within a business is referred to as "tradition." Tradition is for weddings, holidays, and sports teams. Tradition in business, on the other hand, is usually a bad thing (unless you happen to be in a business that relates to weddings, holidays, or sports teams, that is).

A company described as "traditional" is seen as having outdated values and being resistant to change. Traditional organizations can seem impossible to change. They are not. To see why, let's look at what you could call one of the most traditional organizations in the world, which is slowly changing because of the dedicated efforts of a new breed of professionals who are mixing the old with the new in a quest to help their "customers" (patrons) make sense of the digital explosion of content.

The Library 2.0 Movement

David Lee King, by any measure, is a very recognizable kind of techie. His blog, named after himself, features examples of him dabbling with videos that he uploads to YouTube. He has an iPhone, uses Flickr, Second Life, and del.icio.us to manage his digital identity and content, and describes the best way to get in touch with him on his site by sharing his Skype userid and urging people to "text me rather than phone—I'm not usually set up for the phone thing." Yet David is not just another Web 2.0 guy working at a Silicon Valley start-up. He doesn't even work in the technology field, technically. He's the Digital Branch and Services manager at the Topeka and Shawnee County Public Library in Topeka, Kansas.

He is also one among many librarians who have launched their own movement to incorporate more technology into library services, referring to their work as Library 2.0. Changing a library is slow work. Yet librarians around the world are blogging, contributing to wikis, using social media to locate and organize information, and, along the way, reinventing a profession that will very likely be one of the most important of the future.

There was a time when libraries were the conduit to all knowledge and the guardians of history. In recent years, many social commentators have made the argument that the importance of the library has been vastly diminished by the Internet and the increased ability of anyone to obtain any information on demand without venturing far from their high-speed connection. Google's publicly stated mission may be to "organize the world's information," but it is the new librarians that are fulfilling the second part of Google's mission by making it "universally accessible and useful."

Another blogging librarian named Jenny Levine authors a popular blog called The Shifted Librarian where she helps other librarians move ahead, describing the idea of a "shifted librarian" as the new way that information will be consumed in the future in a world where information is completely portable and available when we want it. The following description is from her blog:

A "shifted librarian" is someone who is working to make libraries more portable. We're experimenting with new methods, even if we find out they don't work as well as we thought they would. Sometimes, we're waiting for our colleagues, our bosses, and even the kids to catch up, but we're still out there trying. And please don't think I don't love books and print, because I do. No amount of technology will ever replace them, and libraries will always be a haven for books. It's the extras that I'm concentrating on, especially as we try to serve our remote patrons. So welcome to the online life of a shifted librarian. I'm glad you're coming along for the ride, because it's going to be fun. I promise.

Library 2.0 is challenging traditions and continually gaining more and more ground through the dedicated efforts of individuals who are willing to challenge their own status quo and find new solutions to old problems. Attend any Library 2.0–related conference or gathering and you will see just how much this profession is evolving and how hot of a topic this really is. If libraries can do it, you can too.

Conquering the Tradition Barrier

Traditional organizations are like ships, steadily moving in one direction and allowing inertia to keep them on the same path. Sometimes tradition can actually be one of the easiest barriers to address, depending on your organization, because it is usually followed for only one or two reasons. The first is nostalgia, and the second is because of a mistaken belief that the way business is currently being

GO TO GUIDE p.280

conducted is the best way since it has always worked before (a reason clearly related to the barrier of success described earlier).

If it is nostalgia you are dealing with, a simple honest assessment of why this should not be a barrier and a recommendation for change is really all you can do. Nostalgia can be a deep-rooted barrier, and sometimes it is something that a company simply will not attempt to remove. That's the unfortunate truth. The second reason for tradition is easier to combat because you can use a logical argument against things always having been done a certain way.

Finding a Precedent

If you work in an organization where every new idea is immediately followed by the question "Who has tried this before?" then you understand the fourth barrier: precedent. The one group of people that perhaps better than any other knows precedent is lawyers. Lawyers know it because most of the arguments, written or oral, they make in every case must be backed up by a precedent from a ruling in a previous court case. When many lawyers leave law school, their first job involves researching the scores of previous legal cases to find precedents that can prove a case. "Landmark cases" in the legal world are considered those that set new precedents never seen before, and such cases are rare. That's why those cases are described as "unprecedented" and revered in legal circles. For a lawyer, precedent offers the justification for making an argument. Without it, an argument is usually abandoned.

The problem that many businesses have is that they are stuck in a mode of thinking that makes them feel that they require precedent the same way lawyers do. Yet where the core function of lawyers is to help their clients avoid risk, good marketing often requires a business to embrace it. Your business should not take orders from your lawyer. As Guy

Kawasaki brilliantly suggested in a blog post titled "The Art of Partnering," "The best way to deal with lawyers is to simply say to them: 'This is what I want to do. Now keep us out of jail as we do it.'"[2]

Fight the Copycat Marketers

When businesses focus too much on precedent, it can often lead to what is known adopts copycat marketing. Copycat marketing is where one business adopts the marketing techniques of another, simply because the "copycat" business assumes that if that marketing strategy is working for its competitor the strategy will work for it too. This behavior explains the rush by so many companies in 2006 and early 2007 to build a presence in the virtual world Second Life (without first thinking through their decision strategically). It also explains why all the ads in a particular category in the Yellow Pages look the same. And it explains just about every over-hyped me-too marketing tactic ever tried by unimaginative marketers to cash in on an idea that worked for someone else.

Am I suggesting that you ignore what works for your competition and go your own way? Of course not. Knowing what is working for your competition is something every smart business does. What you need to do is move from thinking in terms of a precedent giving you the right to do something, and consider instead that it is your challenge to think about the right twist on something that can make it effective for your business.

LiveVault—Making Data Storage Fun

The way to market complex technical services to IT managers is through white papers. Anyone who has done business-to-business marketing in the

---

[2] http://blog.guykawasaki.com/2006/02/the_art_of_part.html

tech industry already knows this to be true. The only problem with this approach is that everyone is doing it. So when a company called Iron-Mountain Digital in 2005 had a new solution called LiveVault, which they described as "the industry's first fully automated disk-based backup and recovery solution," it was going to be a tough sell. The reason was that selling it required IT managers to unlearn a commonly held bias (that backing up data by using tape was more reliable) and embrace the belief that a new method of backing up digitally could replace the tape reliably. Cassettes, VHS tapes, and floppy disks are all rapidly dying (if not already dead) methods of storing media using tape—a technology that is more than 50 years-old. Yet when it comes to businesses storing their data, the vast majority of companies still prefer to use either tape or a combination of digital and tape. IronMountain needed a way to make the go digital message stand out more powerfully.

So IronMountain took a risk and decided to skip the traditional business-to-business marketing methods such as speaking at conferences, sponsoring trade show booths, and authoring white papers and decided instead to create the "Institute of Backup Trauma." The institute was a fictional place profiled in a series of online videos starring John Cleese (of Monty Python fame and star of lots of other comedies) as Dr. Harold Twain Weck, the director of the institute.

The institute was run for the benefit of IT managers who had relied on tape-based backup, subsequently lost their company data, and were now being "rehabilitated" at the institute into believers in LiveVault's digital solution. The videos included trademark humor from the brilliant Cleese; poked fun at the company itself, with Cleese (being an obviously paid actor) finishing one short video with the query "Where's my check?"; and included references that only a true IT geek could love (such as having Twain Weck's old boss played by Michael Dorn, the same actor who played

Mr. Worf in *Star Trek: The Next Generation*). Even the tagline telling what the product could do for you was unconventional.

Save your job

Save your sanity

Save your butt

The main film ends with Dr. Weck introducing three buttons and pleading with the user not to click the third button. Of course, that's the one everyone clicks, and it leads to a short additional film segment, and then a form registering one to learn more about LiveVault's solutions.

The video was a viral hit, with more than 100,000 views within the first six weeks (huge for a B2B targeted video), a tenfold increase in site traffic, and thousands of sales leads. The site also won numerous marketing awards. More important, it demonstrated that LiveVault was not your everyday data storage provider and had a different (and better) solution.

Conquering the Precedent Barrier

As the story of LiveVault shows, sometimes taking an approach completely different from what worked for your competition will lead to something that works for you. The best way to think about how to handle this is in terms of a point of reference.

I don't wear a watch, and yet I always know what time it is. How? Because I know at what time I left somewhere, or what time my last meeting ended. I have a point of reference and therefore I can usually guess the time within a few minutes without needing a clock. Ideas are like the time; you always have a starting point that you can relate them to.

To conquer the precedent barrier, you need to find a viable point of reference that you can claim as a precedent and build your idea from there.

LiveVault had white papers and wanted you to read them. The way it got you to them was entirely different. The best ideas are the ones that find the point of reference but stand alone as new and original.

What's Next?

So far we have spoken about how organizations can conquer the four great barriers faced by those who want to inject their brand with personality. In each case, it requires the bold actions of a dedicated individual or individuals who are able to find the authority to motivate their organization to get past its fears. People from any level of an organization can do this.

I have spent my career selling ideas to large companies—and the way that innovative ideas get accepted is always very similar. To get to it, the first thing you need to do is paint a background of action. Pull together information, case studies, stories, and anything else you can find to demonstrate that what you want to do is already happening to some degree. This is about answering the fear of precedent, and also building toward the second thing you need to do, which is establish an imperative to act.

You don't want to simply encourage action, you want to encourage it now. For this to happen there needs to be something impending that makes acting now necessary. This could be competitors planning new things, or a big shift about to happen in your industry. Either way, the imperative has to be for now. Of course, an imperative is too lofty to act on immediately, which is why you need to provide a bite-sized way to start. Redeveloping a Web site is too big of a goal; starting by redesigning one page in a section is easier to accept. The bite-sized approach works and offers you a way to get started right away.

The final element is something that is most often forgotten once you reach action—sharing the credit. This is the last essential step because it makes it likely that the idea will travel further and have more success.

Buy-in is also, in part, about ownership and the more people who feel it, the further you can go.

This method is the best way to help business partners, peers, trusted advisors, and even some of your top customers understand and support the idea of putting more personality into your communications. This puts you in the perfect situation to start doing it. All you need to know now is how to uncover your personality moments, which is what I'll show you in Chapter 6.

The Sellevator Pitch

Fear is the underlying reason behind most of the barriers to personality and manifests itself through success, uncertainty, tradition, and precedent. To overcome these, you need to find a position of authority within your organization (based on respect or authority).

Chapter 6

Add Personality and Stir

Finding and Using Personality Moments

He entered the elevator. "Ground floor, please," he said.
He sounds nice, she thought, but he wouldn't notice me.
He noticed. He noticed her standing there, eyes straight ahead.
But he didn't blame her.
Nice perfume, he thought as they parted,
he lightly stroking his disfigured face,
she counting the steps to the waiting van.

—Chris Macy, "Like Two Ships"

In the late 1980s a fellow named Steve Moss, who published a regional paper called the *New Times* in San Luis Obispo County, California, decided to launch a contest. A self-described lover of words, he called his annual writing challenge the Fifty-five Fiction Contest, because every story entered had to contain exactly 55 words. After nearly a decade of accepting submissions from writers and publishing a winner each year,

Moss published a collection of these winning stories in 1995 and called the compilation *The World's Shortest Stories*. In that year, I first read "Like Two Ships" and more than 10 years later the story has stuck in my head. What made this story so memorable? Is it the romance of two star-crossed lovers, one blind and the other disfigured, who would never meet? The fact that the story contained only 55 words? Actually, it was something far more basic.

The story was memorable because it captured and brought it to life a poignant, subtly dramatic moment that we can all recognize. Who can admit to never having had such a moment in an elevator with someone and thinking "What if?" Now consider this in relation to your business. There are similarly powerful moments that happen every day as you run your business, when you have a chance to build a deeper relationship with your customers, but often the moment passes unnoticed. It is the classic situation of forgetting about the little things while focusing instead on the continual quest for more sales and profits. If all your effort only amounts to selling something and cashing in on the sale, you have a problem. This chapter is about learning to spot the moments in between. Those hidden chances are your personality moments.

Understanding Personality Moments

A *personality moment* is a trigger. It is a point in time when you have the chance to build your relationship with your customer, or when you are in danger of losing it. There is a reason I am introducing the idea of personality moments in this chapter, just before we get to Part Two. So far, we have talked about all the elements that make up your company's personality. We've seen the range of people that can be spokespeople for your brand, and the importance of creating a strong backstory. These are all big things.

Personality moments are the opposite. They are the dozens of small occurrences that happen during an interaction between you and your customer, both before and after you make a sale or provide a service. The fact that these events are small doesn't make them insignificant; it only makes them easier to miss. This collection of small things is what builds the perception of your brand. The last stage of learning to inject more personality into your brand is understanding how to effectively spot and use your personality moments.

All of the examples of companies that I have shared thus far demonstrate the importance of doing this. Oil Can Henry's knows that letting its customers watch while mechanics work on their cars is a personality moment. SCOTTEVEST knows that the moment you get your multipocketed vest and start unzipping and looking in every pocket is a personality moment. Stacy Madison understood that her personality moment was when customers were waiting in line at her fledgling sandwich cart—and taking advantage of the moment actually led to the birth of her company.

 Personality moments are all around us and they represent pivotal moments in which you can build customer loyalty and stand apart from competitors. So let's talk about how you can get better at spotting them.

GO TO GUIDE *p.*283

Desperately Seeking Attention

Another way to define a personality moment is as any moment when you have the attention of a customer or potential customer. This includes when they are researching products or about to purchase from you. It encompasses the time they spend unpacking your product when they get home, and the time they spend reading about it online before buying. You need to have the attention of a customer before you can do anything else.

Of course, attention is the prize that most companies are seeking from their customers or potential customers. In fact, attention is the prize everyone seems to be seeking, which has led to the common pronouncement that we are in an *attention economy*. The brands that dominate our lives and do the best are the ones that are able to capture attention the longest. It is no accident that when we talk about getting someone's attention, we usually talk of "capturing" it. Attention is seen as something to be chased. As we will see later in this chapter, this is exactly the view we need to get away from. Before we talk about that, however, let's take a closer look at how most organizations chase attention today.

The Three Methods of Getting Attention

Every idea you can think of for getting the attention of your customers will fall into one of three broad categories: *shock, sex,* or *relevance*. It may seem too simplistic to narrow it down to just these three things, but if you think about it every other method comes from these. Think of them as you do primary colors. Every way to get attention comes from some combination of these three elements. To say that shock and sex are popular ways of capturing attention today is probably a gross understatement. Everywhere you turn, sex is being used to promote just about everything from fashion and beauty products (just about 100 percent of them) to more surprising uses like the recent campaign from the People for the Ethical Treatment of Animals (PETA) for vegetarianism, featuring print images of a naked Alicia Silverstone, and other stars.

The best examples of using sex to capture attention are those that manage to merge it with a message of relevance. One great example of this is the now-famous series of online videos developed by my colleagues at Ogilvy & Mather in Toronto for Dove skin-care products. The videos were part of Dove's Campaign for Real Beauty and showed young girls being assailed by images of supermodel perfection. The ads still used sex, but merged it with a message of relevance, which was (from a tagline used in the second video called "Onslaught") to "speak to your daughter before the beauty industry does."

When it comes to shock, one of the most riveting examples in recent memory is the series of safety-focused ads for Volkswagen developed by Crispin Porter & Bogusky, in which jarring images of people walking away from split-second accidents were used to show the safety of VW cars. Of course, shock is seldom used this perfectly. Few would argue with the fact that there is no shortage of shock or sex being used today in media or marketing.

In each of these examples of the successful use of sex and shock, the reason for their success is that the sex or shock is coupled with a relevant message. Relevance is the key factor that transforms something from good entertainment to good and entertaining marketing. In most cases, if you manage to entertain your audience but do not generate a benefit for your brand then you have essentially engaged in public service, not a marketing campaign. To a degree, this is what the annual advertising lovefest surrounding the Super Bowl has become—a chance for brands to entertain consumers with questionable linkages back to their brands.

There are thousands of examples of marketing efforts that fit this category. The brands using them manage to capture attention for a moment, but lose it quickly after that. Of the three methods for capturing attention, relevance is clearly the unifying factor that makes a message more than something that simply captures attention for a moment and squanders it after that.

Relevance Is the Key

A perfect illustration of the power of relevance is online keyword marketing. Every artfully written haiku-style text ad for Google is aimed at the same goal—to get someone to click a link. That click is generated through also how effectiveness is typically measured. Click through [...] e the industry standard for performance of an online campaign. Once a user has clicked that link, he or she comes to a superoptimized "landing page," which should be tailor-made for what we believe they were interested in, and from then on the experience is focused on conversion. This is a typical model for what most businesses would likely consider good marketing. Relevance is usually expected to lead to conversion.

The struggle to be relevant, though, is tricky business. Reaching the right person at the right time with the right message is notoriously difficult. If it were easy, you would never need to read a book about how to do it. What is often forgotten is that there *is* one way to get your customers' attention through relevance that doesn't require you to "capture" it. Before you start using personality moments effectively, you need to know what this method is and the paradox that leads to it.

The Attention Paradox

Herbert Simon, the late Nobel laureate economist famously said, "A wealth of information creates a poverty of attention."[1] When it comes to most marketing messages, this is certainly true. An interesting result of our constantly dealing with this wealth of information is that we are all getting better at filtering out information that we don't care about. *The point is not that we have less attention to give, but that we are far more selective with how we spend it.*

Now let's look at this selective attention and apply it to something most businesses will be familiar with: the buying cycle. This is a cycle of activities that typically happens between the moment when consumers are deciding what to buy and the point when they use it and start the process

[1] H. A. Simon, "Designing Organizations for an Information-Rich World," in Martin Greenberger, *Computers, Communication, and the Public Interest*, 1971, pp. 40–41.

over again. With slight variations, it is usually a very similar diagram. Here's my view of what the buying cycle today looks like:

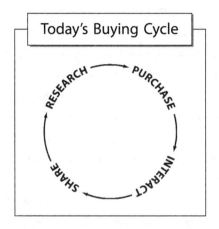

Today's Buying Cycle

RESEARCH → PURCHASE → INTERACT → SHARE

Before I go into detail about each phase, I should note that if you think about our "poverty of attention," it is largely based on looking at the first stage of this cycle: research. This is the stage where the majority of marketing dollars are spent. Brands try to buy ads in places where consumers are likely to look as they seek a particular product or service. Keyword ads on Google are targeted to keywords in searches that people use to research. Public relations efforts focus on media that a target audience is assumed to consume. Whether you realize it or not, the bulk of your time, effort, and budget in marketing is being spent on just one phase of the buying cycle: the first one.

Kill the Silos

You can probably already see where this is going. If the latter three phases of the buying cycle are left largely untouched by marketing dollars, then the natural questions to focus on are why this is and what to do about it. The obvious reason most marketing focuses on just the research stage is that the other phases are handed off to other departments or seen as the responsibility of different teams within an organization (fulfillment, customer service, tech support, etc.). If you have ever worked in an organization with departments like this, you will understand what I mean when I say "kill the silos," meaning, break down the barriers between departments and roles.

When your customer gets to the next stage of purchasing your product or service, she has already made a decision to interact with you and is either in the act of buying it or waiting to buy it. This is followed by the moment when she gets a product or service, opens it, and first uses it. Often concurrently, she is also sharing this experience with others or providing feedback to you.

This is the paradox of attention—that the moment when you have your customer's nearly undivided attention is the same moment when the relationship with the customer moves from marketing to other areas of the business. None of these three moments after research suffers from a paucity[2] of attention. Yet it is often wasted. The real question you need to answer is: how can you start to better focus on those moments where you *already have your customer's attention* and use those to demonstrate your personality?

Forget the Thrill of the Chase

To do this, you first need to forget the thrill of the chase. This is a chase most of us know well, in which consumers are hapless "targets"—and we use every militaristic term we can muster (guerrilla, campaign, target, capture, etc.) to describe the ways in which we try to hunt them down. Yet for all the time organizations spend on this chase, it is almost always a difficult task, because it requires us to find ever-new ways to capture consumers' attention. What if your local pizza delivery chains didn't have to come up with

---

[2] I know I talked about simplicity in writing in Chapter 4, but this is too cool of a word to pass up. I dare you to say it out loud and not be just a little impressed with yourself.

one more new way to stuff double the cheese into some new orifice of a pizza crust in order to "reinvent" pizza? The world would be a simpler place.

In fact, home pizza delivery offers a great example of the dangers of this chase. In recent years the product has been overdramatized by new "innovations" that seem to emerge every few months. These pizza makers are all competing in the research phase of your buying cycle, when you are making your choice about which one to call. What about the moment when the pizza is delivered to you, or when you are eating it, or when you are ordering your next one? These are the forgotten moments in the pizza delivery process, and the ones that are ripe for using personality.

As we will see in the rest of this chapter, the secret to being able to use personality moments effectively is having a good eye for spotting when you have captured your customer's attention and have a chance to do more with it. Your goal should be to more efficiently turn every such situation into a personality moment. The brands that do this successfully are the ones that develop personality.

Throughout the rest of this chapter, you will read examples of brands that are successfully using their personality moments across more than one phase of the buying cycle. We will also look at some case studies of brands that have managed to find and use their personality moments to great effect. In many cases, these brands are focusing on the moments when they have their customer's attention. A few also find a way to stand out from competitors at the point of research and even before purchase or before their brand or products are ever considered. In either case, the ideal method for learning how to recognize personality moments is to study how some of these brands do it—starting with an unlikely choice, one that doesn't really offer a product or a service. The example is a southern rock and roll band that has built a passionate following of fans who they affectionately call the Hazelnuts.

A Rock Boat for Hazelnuts

A rock band is a great place to start exploring how personality moments work, because bands have so many opportunities to have them. Music is an emotional and usually deeply personal experience for people when they truly love a certain kind of music or band. Sister Hazel is a band that knows this better than most. In fact, the band has created such an effective model for building its fan base that its lead singer and manager were invited to participate in a session during the Word of Mouth Marketing Association (WOMMA) Summit in late 2007 to discuss how they do it.

In case you aren't familiar with the band, they have played a unique style of acoustic guitar and southern rock for more than a decade and describe their music as "solid and satisfying, comfortable and easy, like old friends and family." Aside from creating great music, Sister Hazel is a potent example of a brand that cultivates its personality moments; it does this by maintaining an unwavering focus on building a relationship with its fans (whom they call Hazelnuts).

Early in its career, to build a fan base, the band would give away two cassettes for every one that it sold. It created a program called Hazel Virgins, which allowed fans to bring a friend who was not a regular listener to a show for free. In 2002, after many requests from fans for more intimate shows in venues other than megastadiums, Sister Hazel founded the Rock Boat, which became (and still is) the largest floating music festival in the world, attracting hundreds of fans and up to 30 bands performing over the four- to five-day cruise every year.

Yet for all their innovative ways of fostering a relationship with their fans, the most powerful example is a story that lead singer Ken Block shared at the WOMMA event, describing how the band would order pizza and play a few songs for fans who were lined up in the cold waiting to get into a show. Having customers waiting in line for hours is a perfect example of a personality moment that most brands let pass without taking advantage of. For Sister Hazel, it was just another chance to demonstrate how much they cared for and appreciated their fans.

Yet with all of the things that the band does, from Rock Boat to smaller shows and even a snowboarding music festival they pioneered, the story that most people tell and retell, and one that demonstrates what makes this band so different, is the one about the band standing outside in the cold alongside its fans, feeding them and making sure they had something to listen to while they waited.

Of course, you might be thinking that the music industry lends itself to using personality more readily than in your communications. After all, there is never going to be another band that makes exactly the same music as they do, right? So let's look at a completely different category where having a personality seems like the ultimate oxymoron—banking.

ING Direct

Direct banking online is a relatively new trend that is helping millions of people around the world to more easily save money. One of the pioneers of direct banking is ING Direct, which created its first offering back in 1997. Today, ING Direct services are offered in nine different countries to more than 16 million customers. In case you haven't jumped into it yet and opened your own account, direct banking is essentially a method by which banks can offer a savings account online at a higher than usual interest rate as a trade-off for the bank typically not having any physical branches or tellers.

If the cynic in you thinks that this is just another way for banks to save money while still making money from your money, you are probably right on some level. ING Direct, however, has been taking a different approach. Arkadi Kuhlmann is not the typical banking CEO either. He describes his service in a different way than most banks do.

Banking feels like going to the dentist. Life doesn't have to be that complicated. We're not a bank the way you usually think of a bank. The way you interact with us is the way you interact with any retailer you know. Banks have always said the customer is always right, we'll do what the customer wants. You know what that means? That means it costs everyone a bundle. Making savings cool is what we're about. That's what we want to accomplish. There is nothing more empowering than some money you consider to be your own.

Does this sound like the usual description of what a bank can do for you? The stated aim of ING Direct is to make banking easy and help you save your money. Kuhlmann does a good job of demonstrating the personality of the bank to customers, but the real personality moments for the bank come through its interactions with its customers.

The bank is a sponsor of many smart marketing campaigns, including offering free transit to a day to commuters in cities like Washington, D.C., and San Francisco. It also sponsors the New York City Marathon and many other regional events, which helps position the brand as more than just virtual.

In several cities, you might even find an ING Café—a retail destination designed to look nothing like the branch of a bank. Every touch, from the décor to the chairs is designed like a café. Early on, ING realized that despite running a virtual banking business, customers still wanted to see something physical; hence the café concept was born. What ING Direct manages to do with every interaction is treat it as a moment to exhibit the company's personality, which is irreverent, open, friendly, and genuine. In short, everything that you would never expect from a bank.

As a result, ING boasts a stunning 96 percent customer satisfaction rate (unheard of in the banking industry) and continues to acquire more and more customers every day. ING Direct proves that even in a business as staid as banking, there is a place for personality.

Personality Hotels

Aside from a few exceptions like ING Direct, most consumers would place financial services companies at the bottom of the list of industries whose brands develop personality effectively. Hotels would likely be at the opposite end of the list. In the past 10 years, the personality of a hotel has become more and more of a motivating factor in people's choice of where to stay. A major sign of this trend was a small paperback book called *Hip Hotels* published in 1999, which generated worldwide sales far beyond all expectations.

As its title suggests, the book was dedicated to profiling cool hotels around the world for people seeking a unique, nonstandardized hotel experience. As it turned out, that group of consumers was bigger than anyone expected. The book turned into a series, and then into a Web site. To date, the series includes more than 14 books, has sold more than 2 million copies, and the books have been translated into 10 languages. The Web site for the books features custom photographs of each of the profiled hotels (containing images much clearer than the usual blurry amateur photographs found on most small-hotel Web sites) and the site features a link whereby you can search for hotels that have been profiled in the book and directly make a reservation at any one of them around the world.

If you happened to be searching for hip hotels in San Francisco, one particularly interesting one comes up, the Hotel Diva. The Diva is part of a group of six hotels all clustered around Union Square in downtown San Francisco. Each of these six hotels has a distinct personality and character all its own. These personalities, in fact, are so central to what each hotel has to offer that it is reflected in the name of the entire group: Personality Hotels.

For anyone who has stayed at a Personality Hotel, there are a few features that will likely stand out. At the Hotel Diva, there are four custom-designed suites that you can tour and a distinctly intimate ambiance throughout the hotel. At the Hotel Union Square (built in 1913 and one of the oldest art deco hotels in San Francisco), you can stay in the same suite where author Dashiell Hammett used to stay. Each hotel has a distinct personality that will not appeal to everyone. But it works for Personality Hotels.

One of the most talked about personality moments at the Hotel Diva, however, has nothing to do with the design or décor. Instead it involves the way that the hotel adds its own twist to something few hotel guests ever pay attention to (unless something goes wrong)—the comment card. At all Personality Hotels, this is known as the Picasso Comment Card and each of these includes a drawing of a stick figure that you can customize to your own specifications while you answer a few simple questions. (See page 173.)

Everything about the experience at Personality Hotels is meant not only to demonstrate the personality of the brand, but also to help you find and explore your own personality. As the dozens of comment cards they have posted online demonstrate, people have an experience at the hotels that they are unable to stop talking about and sharing with others.

Hundreds of other "hip hotels" as well as hotels that may not have made this list are also projecting personality worldwide, using their individuality as a competitive advantage. Starwood, one of the largest hotel

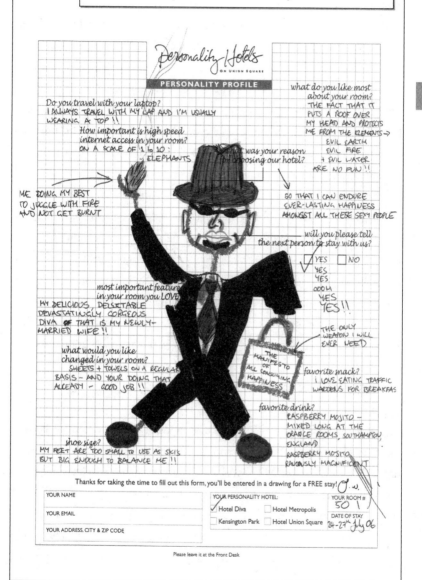

Personality Hotels
ON UNION SQUARE

PERSONALITY PROFILE

Do you travel with your laptop?
I ALWAYS TRAVEL WITH MY LAP AND I'M USUALLY
WEARING A TOP !!

*How important is high speed
internet access in your room?*
ON A SCALE OF 1 6 10 :
~ ELEPHANTS

*what do you like most
about your room?*
THE FACT THAT IT
PUTS A ROOF OVER
MY HEAD AND PROTECTS
ME FROM THE ELEMENTS →
EVIL EARTH
EVIL FIRE
+ EVIL WATER
ARE NO FUN !!

*...t was your reason
...hoosing our hotel?*
SO THAT I CAN ENDURE
EVER-LASTING HAPPINESS
AMONGST ALL THESE SEXY PEOPLE

ME DOING MY BEST
TO JUGGLE WITH FIRE
AND NOT GET BURNT

*will you please tell
the next person to stay with us?*
☑ YES ☐ NO
YES
YES
OOOH
YES
YES !!

*most important feature
in your room you LOVE*
MY DELICIOUS, DELECTABLE
DEVASTATINGLY GORGEOUS
DIVA OF THAT IS MY NEWLY-
MARRIED WIFE !!

THE
MANIFESTO
OF
ALL CONSUMING
HAPPINESS

THE ONLY
WEAPON I WILL
EVER NEED

*what would you like
changed in your room?*
SHEETS + TOWELS ON A REGULAR
BASIS - AND YOUR DOING THAT
ALREADY - GOOD JOB !!

favorite snack?
I LOVE EATING TRAFFIC
WARDENS FOR BREAKFAS

favorite drink?
RASPBERRY MOJITO -
MIXED LONG AT THE
ORANGE ROOMS, SOUTHAMPTON
ENGLAND
RASPBERRY MOJITO
RAUCOUSLY MAGNIFICENT

shoe size?
MY FEET ARE TOO SMALL TO USE AS SKIS
BUT BIG ENOUGH TO BALANCE ME !!

Thanks for taking the time to fill out this form, you'll be entered in a drawing for a FREE stay!

YOUR NAME

YOUR EMAIL

YOUR ADDRESS. CITY & ZIP CODE

YOUR PERSONALITY HOTEL:
☑ Hotel Diva   ☐ Hotel Metropolis
☐ Kensington Park ☐ Hotel Union Square

YOUR ROOM #
50 1

DATE OF STAY
24-27ᵗʰ July 06

Please leave it at the Front Desk

brands in the world, has long used design at their W Hotel chain to express a personality that is different from what you might expect from a chain. Aside from a distinctive design using dark browns, blues and reds, some locations also feature Chinese checkers boards in some rooms, and green apples in the front lobby. Starwood's soon-to-be launched new hotel brand, called "aloft," first tested its concept and personality in virtual world Second Life in 2006 and is set to open near Boston and in Beijing in July 2008. Even the Doubletree brand, which would rarely be mistaken for a hip hotel, has created its own personality moment by offering guests a fresh-baked chocolate chip cookie on arrival.

So far you may have noticed that the examples of Sister Hazel, ING Direct, and Personality Hotels all feature physical presences and real moments in which employees are interacting with customers and there are face-to-face moments when these brands can demonstrate their personalities. Although personality moments do frequently happen in person, they can just as often happen online as well. To understand how, we can look at an example of a company that uses the time customers spend visiting their Web site and shopping online to create its own personality moments.

Selling Bike Messenger Personality

More than a decade ago, an obnoxious bigoted cast member of one of the first-ever reality TV shows inspired thousands of kids to dream of becoming bike messengers. As any member of Generation X will likely remember, *The Real World* on MTV was a hallmark moment in television. It put seven strangers into a house together and taped their experience. Though the program still runs today, its third season in 1994 remains the one that most people will remember, because of two unforgettable characters. The first was Pedro Zamora, an openly gay, Cuban-American HIV-positive

AIDS educator whom President Bill Clinton once credited with humanizing and putting a face on the disease of HIV and AIDS at a time when there was little understanding about the condition. The second was an insensitive, slovenly San Francisco bike messenger named David "Puck" Rainey.

By all accounts, Puck could very well have been the most disgusting human anyone had ever seen on television. He picked his nose and scabs all the time, and farted with pride. Still, his casting in the program was a brilliant choice as he made compelling television with the conflicts he created. His insanely dangerous bike rides weaving through San Francisco traffic inspired a generation of kids to look at the job of bike messenger as the ultimate way to get paid for an adventurous job. In part, due to the popularity of *The Real World*, the popularity of the urban bike messenger culture took off as well.

One of the most popular pieces of gear from the bike messenger was the messenger bag—a one-strap alternative to the dorkier two-strap backpacks everyone had been using for decades. Around the same time that Puck was darting through traffic and almost getting run over, a small company was producing durable bags for bike messengers out of a warehouse in San Francisco and was starting to get a reputation among young urbanites for its hip and authentic bags.

The company was called Timbuk2 and its distinctive three-panel design and swirl logo on its messenger bags quickly became a fashion icon in the Bay Area far beyond the subculture of bike messengers. Today, the personality of the brand is evident in how it describes itself.

Timbuk2 is more than a bag. It's more than a brand. Timbuk2 is a bond. To its owner, a Timbuk2 bag is a dependable, everyday companion. We see fierce, emotional attachments form between Timbuk2 customers and their bags all the time. A well-worn Timbuk2 bag has a certain patina—the stains and scars of everyday urban adventures.

The most interesting aspect of Timbuk2, however, is not this description on its Web site or even the authentic heritage of the brand, but rather how it uses the online medium to demonstrate its personality as part of its buying process. This happens as soon as someone makes it to the Timbuk2 site and sees the messages about the rugged durability of the bags and bike messenger heritage that led to the company's founding.

To engage its customers, the site offers a "People Powered Customer Service" option whereby customers can answer one another's questions or interact directly and immediately with Timbuk2 staff during a purchase. The company hand stitches its bags in San Francisco, and shares openly online that it had to move production of its laptop bags offshore because they are more complex to make. Everything about the experience online with Timbuk2 is designed to bring you into the personality of the brand and interact with it.

Of course, we cannot discuss the purchasing cycle without also looking at the moment of evaluation during which consumers are comparing one product with another. Nowhere is this comparison more pronounced than in a grocery store, where products are put on display right next to one another within reach of consumers, who can see and read everything about the product. This is the market in which Innocent Drinks, a maker of fruit smoothies in the UK, has managed to create their own memorable personality moment.

Innocent Drinks

If you walk into a Sainsbury retail grocery store in the UK during the winter, you will see a curious type of product lining the shelves in the chilled beverage section. All of the bottles of fruit smoothies made by a company called Innocent Drinks will be wearing small woolen hats—all with different designs. Look a bit closer and you will find that those hats are knitted by volunteers and that if you buy any of those bottles with the small hat on top, a donation will be made to a charity called Age Concern. Why these curious hats and this strange choice of charity for Innocent Drinks? As cofounder Richard Reed describes it, the brand "simply wanted to develop a product where the image matched the product." Clearly, the image of Innocent Drinks was meant to be something out of the ordinary.

The drinks are called innocent because they are fresh, use real fruits, and have no added sugar or concentrates. In a series of powerful TV spots, Innocent Drinks shows a pile of fruit next to a bottle of its product and the fruit disappears to demonstrate that the entire pile of fruit (and nothing else) goes into one of their smoothies. The product clearly has a story that people can associate with, but the experience it manages to create only begins with the product. Its Web site invites consumers to "pop in for a cup of tea and a chat"—and it is clear they mean it.

It was this openness toward chatting with customers that led to the idea of the Big Knit in 2003. This is a project that has knitters from around the UK taking up the challenge of knitting little woolly hats to be sold for 50 pence each to raise money for Age Concern, a charity dedicated to helping older people across the UK stay warm in the winter. In 2006, knitters donated more than 230,000 hats and the target for 2007 was 400,000 (which was passed in late November). The Big Knit allows Innocent Drinks to take advantage of its retail personality moment sitting on the shelf at the store waiting to be purchased.

Another way the company takes advantage of the retail environment is by offering chillers covered in artificial grass and daisies to retailers. In the description of these, it promises that there is "no lawn mower required (and guaranteed not to attract any cows)." The rest of their Web site features similar jokes. As Richard Reed notes, "our drinks are totally natural and as a business, we pride ourselves on always being ourselves—open, honest and natural. Our brand voice is a direct reflection of the way we speak and who we are."

This belief is evident in every way that Innocent Drinks communicates. Even its disclaimer for the product's tendency to ferment if left out (remember, it's fresh) is unique.

> Warm smoothies just don't cut the mustard, so as a reminder to those of you who'll be buying our little drinks, please make sure they're kept chilled. If you leave them out of the fridge, they will eventually start to ferment. This is a completely safe, natural process but it means the smoothie goes fizzy.
>
> Sometimes, in cases of rapid fermentation, there will be a build up of gas. Our caps are designed to vent this excess gas, but in some rare occasions, the bottle becomes hard or bloated. In that case, we wouldn't advise opening the bottle in your car, at your desk or in your best cashmere sweater, as it may misbehave and squirt smoothie all over you. Instead, please open over a sink with the cap pointing away from you.
>
> In very rare cases, the cap has been known to pop off all on its own and this can cause a bit of a mess in your fridge. Please let us know immediately if this happens and we will of course help clean up the mess.

As their disclaimer proves, aside from taking advantage of personality moments in retail with their little hats, Innocent Drinks also creates its own unique moments in unexpected places. Another way it does that is through a fleet of Cow Vans and Grass Vans (both decorated vans that employees drive around cities and from which they sell or give away products). Every year toward the end of summer, the brand also puts on an outdoor festival in London's Regent's Park called "FruitStock."

Perhaps the most significant personality moment that Innocent gets right is evident from its customers' response to the last question on a page of frequently asked questions on its Web site, which reads: "I have a question and need a human being to answer it." The company's response is to contact Charlotte from its team, and her contact details are provided.

The Fifth Phase: Indifference

One of the things that you may have noticed about the Innocent Drinks story is that a key personality moment for the brand (when its bottles are on a shelf wearing little woolly hats) is not easily described by one of the four phases of the buying cycle: if someone visiting her local Sainsbury is not looking specifically to buy some type of beverage. The four-phase buying cycle accurately reflects what it is meant to, the phases of *buying*. There is a phase, however, that comes before buying, research, and even before consideration—the phase of indifference.

This phase includes all the moments when someone is not in the buying cycle at all. They are indifferent because they don't care about you or what you have to offer. They are simply not in the market for what you are selling. As common wisdom goes in marketing, this group of consumers who is not in the market for what you have to offer is the toughest to reach. In the past, marketers have done their best by using interruptive marketing messages, but enlightened brands today already understand this will not work. So, what do you do in this fifth stage, where relevance is hardest to inject because it cannot be applied to a specific need? To answer that question, let's look at one of the most watched viral videos on YouTube for a product from the past year, a simple series of videos asking a surprisingly compelling question: will it blend?

The company behind these videos was Blendtec and the videos feature a guy in a white lab coat who takes all kinds of products like CDs, iPods, chickens, iPhones, and more, and sticks them into a Blendtec blender to answer the question of the program—will it blend? The videos are one of the most popular branded video series on YouTube and, more important, they have created a need among some people to get a new blender from Blendtec, even though they may not have realized the need before. The personality moment for a Blendtec blender comes at some point while you are watching it slice through the casing of an iPhone and the smoke is rising. By the way, they suggest you don't try that at home.

The Science of Personality Moments
So far in this chapter, we have seen many examples of brands or businesses that are using their personality moments effectively. One question that may have come up in reading about this diverse range of examples

---

Create Something Talkable

the trick to marketing is to have something so cool, you'd want to talk about it EVEN if you weren't in the business.....

hugh '07

---

is, what ties them all together? Your first clue can probably be taken from the drawing, on page 180, which points to one of the central truths of marketing. Creating something talkable inherently empowers your product or service. Remember the lesson I shared in the Introduction about what personality can and cannot do for your business? It cannot create a star out of a product or service that no one wants. As we have seen, talkability can come from more than just a product itself. There are some products, like the Nintendo Wii or the Apple iPhone, that tend to generate this type of talkability on the sheer power of their innovation.

As consumer evangelists become more common, brands need to find a way to create talkable hooks that inspire these evangelists to discuss the brand. When consumers demand more authenticity, the only way to respond is to find ways to share the real story behind your product or brand. This is not about getting bigger or getting smaller. This is not even about finding something to stand for. This is about understanding what the underlying personality of your brand is, and finding the right moments to use it.

The Sellevator Pitch

Focusing on personality moments means making better use of the times when you already have your customers' attention (during and after purchase) as well as using your personality to attract attention during the other phases.

INTERMISSION

IF YOU TALKED TO PEOPLE
THE WAY ADVERTISING
TALKED TO PEOPLE, THEY'D
PUNCH YOU IN THE FACE.

©hugh

PART TWO

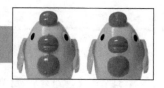

The Butler Was a Marketer

Putting Personality Into Action

Have you skipped straight to this section without reading Part One? For those of you who did, I have one thing to say to you—I probably would too. Business books are not like novels. If you find out the butler did it before reading the rest of a murder mystery, your experience is ruined. In a book like *Personality Not Included*, you can read it in any order you choose, a point I shared at the very beginning of this book as the "nonobvious" way to read it.

The ultimate goal of this book is to be useful, and if you have read Part One, you know that Part Two is meant to offer you everything you will need to apply the ideas presented earlier to your business.

A Recap of *PNI* in Fewer Than 60 Words

Whether you decided to read Part One first or plan to return to it later, the best way to start this section is to have a lightning-fast recap of what we have learned so far.

> **Chapter 1**—Faceless used to work because big meant credible. This is no longer true.
>
> **Chapter 2**—Accidental spokespeople are speaking for your brand. Embrace them.

Chapter 3—*Uniqueness* plus *Authenticity* plus *Talkability* equals *personality*. Use the UAT Filter.

Chapter 4—Backstories establish a foundation of credibility. You need one.

Chapter 5—Fear of change leads to barriers. Finding your authority overcomes them.

Chapter 6—Personality moments are everywhere and unexpected, but you must spot them.

The key theme from Part One is that **personality matters,** because it is the element of your brand that inspires loyalty more than any product feature or element of your service ever can.

The Situational Relevance Test

The fact that there is a Part Two makes this book different from most other business books. The idea of a resource guide in a book, though, is not unheard of. The one thing that causes most business books, even those with elements like a resource guide, to lose or obscure their usefulness is that they never make it clear how their premise can be applied to different situations. This is the situational relevance test, which determines whether or not the theory of a book can be easily applied to your situation. You wouldn't spend a day teaching a man how to fish if he lives in the desert, would you?

In this book, I would have failed the situational relevance test if I spent all of its pages trying to convince you that your business needs to have a personality (which *is* actually what I am telling you)—but never relating this broad directive to your unique situation. Until I do that, it won't be empowering for you.

I cannot tell you to implement all of the ideas in this section from start to finish, because every idea won't work for every type of business.

Instead, Part Two is meant to make personality relevant whether you are an entrepreneur starting your own business, the head of a large team or company, or working in a corporate position with dozens of layers above you on the decision-making tree.

How to Use This Section

As I stated at the outset of this book, Part Two will be divided into two types of resources.

1. **Techniques.** These are essentially styles of marketing. They are meant to inspire your creative thinking and give you real examples of how companies are bringing their personalities to life in a way other than just relying on authentic spokespeople or crafting a smart backstory. If you think of these techniques as the building blocks of personality, then they can help you bring this foundation to life in more creative and promotional ways. There is no limit to the possible number of techniques; that only 10 are discussed is simply a factor of space.

2. **Guides and Tools.** This section relates to each chapter in Part One and offers the step-by-step plans you need to take the suggestions from earlier in the book and put them into action. The section to associate with the chapters from Part One, and the visual bookmarking (explained on page 16) and page references will help you flip back and forth between these guides and the related sections in Part One.

All the resources in this section are focused on situations, which means that if you return to this book after your role has changed (new job, new business, etc.), the lessons should be useful in a different way.

TECHNIQUES

New Styles of Marketing

The techniques presented in this section are meant to be quick tutorials for how to bring your personality to life with different styles of marketing. Techniques are stylized ways of marketing. Those discussed here represent a variety of approaches that will allow you to inject more personality into your company.

The best way to use these techniques is to think of them as action or campaign starters. They are the tools that will develop personality within your organization.

The 10 techniques I will illustrate are not an exhaustive list, but rather a compilation of some of the most powerful ones being used by brands today to great effect. Why should these 10 matter any more than others? They don't; they are simply a starting point. Using techniques like these in marketing is a creative exercise, and it is impossible to say there can be only 10 creative solutions to a problem. To help you identify which of these techniques may be best for your situation, they will be consistently presented in the following format:

1. What is it?
2. Why does it work?
3. When should you use it?
4. Who's doing it?
5. How to do it, step by step

In reading about who is using each technique, you will see that the campaigns of many companies are used as examples. So far, I have not included much about marketing campaigns or how they relate to the underlying brand of an organization. In the worst cases, they don't relate at all. Yet the way that personality often comes to life is through something small and concentrated, like a marketing campaign. It makes sense, therefore, that many of the examples that show how marketers are using these techniques come from the campaigns that they run. Campaigns are also the place where many brands can find the ideal forms and identifiers for what they want their essential personality to be.

For a complete list of techniques, including bonus techniques not included here, visit www.personalitynotincluded/techniques.

OVERVIEW OF TECHNIQUES

CURIOSITY MARKETING	Engaging customers by inspiring their curiosity
KARMIC MARKETING	Doing something good without any expectation of reward
PARTICIPATION MARKETING	Participating in a dialogue without needing to lead it

UN-WHATEVER MARKETING	Positioning your brand or product as the opposite of everything else

SENSORY MARKETING	Using the underutilized senses to promote your business

ANTIMARKETER MARKETING	Making fun of marketing or business to position your brand/product above it

FALLIBILITY MARKETING	Turning mistakes into moments to demonstrate your personality

INSIDER MARKETING	Giving consumers special access to inside information or experiences

INCIDENTAL MARKETING	Taking a small incidental element of your business and marketing it

USEFUL MARKETING	Creating content that has value and using it for marketing

Curiosity Marketing

What Is It?

To describe curiosity marketing, I'm going to use three simple words, but in order to decipher them, you need to follow these instructions:

10th word, line 3, page 27

3rd word, line 8, page 76

11th word, line 21, page 149

Did you figure it out? Curiosity marketing is about using the element of mystery to get people interested in hearing or seeing what you have for them. It is about *making someone look*. If I tell you not to push a button, the first thing you will do is push it. That's human nature, and is just one example of our natural curiosity. We just want to see what happens, and this turns out to be an irresistible impulse.

You may be thinking that using curiosity in marketing could easily become dishonest and inauthentic. That's true. But curiosity marketing is not about intentionally misleading someone or making false promises. The marketing has to *actually* pay off. It is about using the natural human emotion of curiosity to encourage people to engage with your brand or product in a memorable way.

Why Does It Work?

- **Unique.** It uses a natural human emotion that most find irresistible.
- **Authentic.** It demonstrates that you are willing to communicate in a personal, noncorporate way.
- **Talkable.** It creates an interest that people who are engaged will tell others about.

WHEN SHOULD YOU USE IT?

Green Light: When It Works	Red Light: When to Avoid It
It builds awareness for a product or service that relatively few people understand, and/or encourages potential customers to try the product. It is also good for creating intrigue and anticipation about a product or service that has become commonplace.	It can backfire if it ends up creating a barrier between customers and information that they are seeking. You need to be careful in your quest to use curiosity so that you don't sacrifice usability and simplicity.

Who's Doing It?

1. **PostSecret.** One of the most popular blogs online today is a site that rarely gets the credit it deserves—hidden among blogs dominated by business, politics, or consumer electronics. Since 2005, Frank Warren has been publishing PostSecret, a blog on which he posts homemade postcards that people have sent him containing secrets that they have never shared with anyone else. Visiting the site for the first time will awaken your curiosity, because you cannot help but be drawn into reading the postcards. It is a voyeuristic experience that is so deeply real and personal that it is hard not to spend hours on the site. PostSecret has inspired a vibrant community as well. In bookstores

around the world, the latest PostSecret book, *A Lifetime of Secrets,* often has people putting their own secret postcards into the pages of an unpurchased book for someone else to discover and send in to the site.

2. **iPod Shuffle.** When the first iPod Shuffle came out, all the marketing messages pointed to the power of "randomness" as the underlying principle behind why people would like the product. In a world where you can overly script just about everything, wouldn't it be nice to not know what song is going to play next? Randomness drives curiosity and curiosity drives engagement. The iPod Shuffle had a built-in curiosity that helped sell it to a group of consumers who wanted to load their own songs into it, but be surprised by which ones played and in what order. As their marketing claimed, "Random is the new order."

Curiosity Marketing, Step by Step

1. **Assess the situation.** Curiosity doesn't work in a simple question-answer situation, where a customer is looking for something in particular, either a product or some type of information. In these situations, you need to give them an answer that satisfies their query, without distracting them. For any other situation, there can be a place for curiosity.

2. **Find the true curiosity.** The toughest part of using curiosity is understanding that it is not usually tied to a product feature or attribute. You may think that a customer would be curious about how you manufacture your product or about some other element that is interesting to you and your employees, but most don't care. True curiosity is a more basic play on human emotion. It is wanting to know what happens next because your inter-

est has been piqued. Resist the urge to focus on a product benefit and find the true curiosity first.

3. **Create the curiosity.** There are three main methods you can use to create the curiosity.
   - *Hidden Payoff.* This is the idea of a quest, which the customer has to go on in order to realize the hidden payoff.
   - *Randomizer.* This involves presenting content completely at random to keep interest as people stay engaged just to see what will come next.
   - *Forbidden Secret.* Everyone wants to know the thing that they are not supposed to know. The more forbidden, the better.

4. **Help it travel.** Using curiosity in marketing is inherently talkable, because it is different. A key part of your thinking once you create the curiosity is finding ways to help it travel. This may mean encouraging people to do so, or providing specific tools and features (either online or offline) to help them do it.

5. **Measure the right elements.** Curiosity, like many of the other techniques presented in this section, is not meant to be a conversion tool, but rather should be used for engagement. Consequently, measuring a sales spike or related data will not be a good metric for success. Instead, you need to focus on elements like viral discussions seeded, pass-along, or length of engagement.

Karmic Marketing

What Is It?

Karma, in case you happen to be unfamiliar with the concept, is the idea that what you do today will somehow come back and affect what happens to you tomorrow in an unpredictable way. Positive deeds lead to positive outcomes and negative lead to negative. This is not the same thing as *cause* marketing, which is about picking a social cause and supporting it on an organizational level by investing time or money. Karmic marketing is a one-to-one interaction between someone within your organization and someone outside of it. It may be related to a larger cause, such as fighting illiteracy, but it could just as easily be something kind that someone on your team does for a customer to help them get through their day.

Does the thought of doing something kind for a customer unrelated to your business seem odd? It will for many companies. The tricky thing about this technique is that it is a difficult thing to explain to an organization that is focused on measurement and metrics (as most are). Karmic marketing is not focused on conversion or one-to-one results. It means that you need to trust in the fact that when you do something good, a benefit comes back to your brand (or yourself) somehow at some point—even though you may not be able to measure it directly.

Why Does It Work?

- **Unique.** Unfortunately for the world, doing something good for your customers without expecting a return *is* unique because it is so rare.
- **Authentic.** Karmic marketing is all about humanity—showing yours and proving you are not faceless.
- **Talkable.** Any customer on the receiving end of something kind that you do will almost certainly share it with others as they talk about your business.

WHEN SHOULD YOU USE IT?

Green Light: When It Works	Red Light: When to Avoid It
If you have already established a pattern of caring for your customers, then you can authentically try this technique without it seeming contrived.	Do not use this technique when you are not able to get past the lack of direct measurability or do not have a strong enough relationship with your customers so that something like this will not seem out of place.

Who's Doing It?

1. **Zappos.com.** Anyone who has ordered from Zappos.com (the world's largest online shoe store) already knows about its liberal return policy and huge selection of shoes. For many new customers of Zappos, however, the first mention they heard of the brand was in a story that had little to do with shoes. In July 2007, a customer named Zaz Lamarr purchased several pairs of shoes for her mother, who was suffering from an illness and had lost a lot of weight. When Zappos followed up with her on the shoes, she replied that her mother had died and she had not had a chance to return the shoes yet. Zappos immediately scheduled a UPS pickup for the shoes so that she wouldn't have to worry about it, and credited the money back to her. Sometime

later, Zappos also sent the customer a big bouquet of flowers in sympathy. Lamarr, a writer and blogger was moved by Zappos's kindness and talked about the situation on her blog in a post titled "I Heart Zappos".[1] It quickly became viral, and got profiled in blogs and media around the world and generated hundreds of comments, many from people online who now vowed to try Zappos. The lesson? Sometimes just showing your humanity is the best kind of marketing you can do.

Karmic Marketing, Step by Step

1. **Actually care!** I positioned karmic marketing as a "technique," which may strike you as a cold or calculating way of describing a kind act only as a means directed to an end. You should not approach it like this because more than any other marketing technique, using karma means that you actually need to care about doing something good. If you approach this method simply as a technique to be used, you will eventually be uncovered as inauthentic and do more damage to your brand than good.

2. **Empower your employees.** The power of karmic marketing comes from employees acting like kind and decent people. It is not something that can be mandated from the top, and so the all-important first step is to create an environment where employees are rewarded for taking matters into their own hands.

3. **Be authentic.** Consumers are better than ever at sniffing out inauthentic behavior. As a result, karmic marketing can be dangerous to engage in because many consumers will be unlikely

[1] http://www.zazlamarr.com/blog/?p=240

to believe that your organization is truly doing something without the expectation of some kind of reward. The only way to get around this is to be up front about what you are doing. In Zappos' case, the company did what made sense for its business (i.e., issuing a refund and picking up the shoes) and went the extra step by sending flowers. If it had told the customer to keep the shoes, for example, the story would have been far less powerful and seen more as a calculated effort.

4. **Don't go dark (i.e., follow up).** When you do something that demonstrates you care, you cannot cross the act off a list and close the case. Most actions in karmic marketing forge a bond between an employee and the customer. This is not a numbers-based relationship; it is a personal one that requires follow-up.

5. **Let WOM happen, modestly.** The most powerful thing you can do if your karmic marketing action gets recognized and discussed is to let the discussion happen naturally. Understand that some people will see the negative and assume that you are only acting out of a profit-based motivation, but usually you will find other customers who come to your defense if your actions were truly "karmic." Most of the time, you just need to be patient and secure enough to let the conversation happen.

6. **Think long term.** Many times, the benefits of your actions may take a long time to develop. The idea of karma is that there is always an effect; it is just a matter of time. So if you don't see something directly attributable to your action, it is likely that something is happening outside your capacity to measure. This is where patience and faith come in—patience that you will see a benefit, and faith that perhaps you already are seeing one, even if you cannot see it visibly or measure it directly.

Participation Marketing

What Is It?

Participation marketing is not about starting a blog or creating something ownable and branded on the hottest new social network. Instead, it means being a part of something that is already happening among your customers. It is about joining conversations rather than leading them. It is about actively listening instead of just monitoring, and about adding value rather than "leveraging" it.

The easiest way to think about this is as if your business was about to join a soccer game. The worst way to join would be to jump into the game uninvited, hoard the ball trying to demonstrate how great your ball control is, and score goals alone so that everyone will admire you. The best way is to ask for permission to join the game, play the position at which the team most needs you, and prove your skills by participating. Very quickly, you will find that the team will realize (without your needing to display it) just how good your skills are and what position you belong in. Soccer is like most conversations out there—there is already a game happening and the key is to join it in the right way.

Why Does It Work?

- **Unique.** Participating in a conversation means you are willing to have a unique individual voice, which already sets you apart from many of your competitors.
- **Authentic.** When you add your voice to a trusted community and participate, it can carry more weight than any marketing message could.
- **Talkable.** There is no way not to pass the test for talkability when you are having a dialogue.

WHEN SHOULD YOU USE IT?

Green Light: When It Works	Red Light: When to Avoid It
It works best when you use it in an environment where people are already discussing your brand or your industry. Participation marketing does not mean creating a new conversation, but entering into one that is already happening.	This can be a dangerous approach in closed environments that expressly forbid any interaction or participation from brands and companies. It should also be avoided if the people who are participating on behalf of your organization cannot be granted enough authority to actually act on conversations or continue them once they start.

Who's Doing It?

1. **Starwood.** William Sanders has been an active member of one of the largest frequent flyer communities online for more than seven years, a site called FlyerTalk. He has posted more than 15,000 messages (an average of more than five per day) and is one of the most respected members of the FlyerTalk community. In fact, you might not be able to distinguish him from any other enthusiastic traveler on the site, except for one key difference: he works for Starwood and his user name is "Starwood Lurker." Everyone on the site knows immediately that he is affili-

ated with Starwood and this actually cements his credibility instead of diminishing it. He is listening on behalf of Starwood, offering suggestions, helping people resolve their complaints, and has been cited by several frequent travelers and FlyerTalk users as the sole reason why they use Starwood for all their hotel stays.

2. **Dell.com.** As discussed in Chapter 2, Dell has received accolades from the media and blogosphere for how it has managed to turn its culture of inaction into one of engagement and conversation. Key to this has been the way that Dell has empowered its team members to read everything online it can find about Dell, and comment on it. As a result, many of the blog posts you find today that talk about Dell receive (within a day of posting) a comment from someone who works at Dell. If you want to demonstrate participation, there is no greater method than simply reading what people are saying about you on blogs and responding authentically and consistently. Dell, of course, has branded entities like its Web site and blog. Arguably, one of the factors most responsible for its turnaround is not its own ability to create branded sites like IdeaStorm or Direct2Dell, but its willingness to participate openly and consistently in conversations that others are having on other sites.

Participation Marketing, Step by Step

1. **Identify the conversations to participate in.** The first step in participation marketing is obviously to find the right conversations. Online, this may mean message boards, groups on social networks, forums, or prominent blogs. Offline, this could include events, small interest groups, retail interactions, or community

gatherings. The point is to determine all the key situations where conversations relating to your brand or your industry commonly occur and then to isolate the most influential ones.

2. **Appoint a chief listening officer.** To really do participation marketing right, you need to make it someone's ultimate responsibility. This does not necessarily mean that he or she will be the one doing everything, but selecting someone to own it makes it much more likely that it will happen. Using what may seem like an overinflated title like this can also help indicate the importance of this role and also reminds you that the person in this role should share in the results of conversations with the senior management of your organization.

3. **Empower everyone in your organization.** Like other techniques, the key to this one is empowering the people within your organization to have these conversations on your behalf. This means giving everyone the right guidelines for what they can and cannot talk about online, and allowing them to resolve issues on your behalf.

4. **Keep the conversation going.** Participation is an ongoing process, and therefore the last step in this process requires that you have a model in place to actively watch follow-up conversations and keep the dialogue happening with customers. Starting a conversation and then disappearing is the worst thing you can do, because you have already raised expectations by starting a dialogue that you are now obliged to meet.

Un-Whatever Marketing

What Is It?

Un-whatever marketing means defining your service or product based on what you *are not* rather than what you are. In every category, there are typical offerings. Despite how it may sound, typical is not the same thing as bad. Typical can be highly useful. It means that what you offer performs as expected and delivers a result that meets your customers' expectation. The problem with typical is that it also means you have a lot of competition.

When you define yourself as the opposite of something, you can create a conflict that gets people interested. As Robyn Waters pointed out in her most recent trend book, *The Hummer and the Mini,* every trend today seems to have an equal and opposing trend, which she labels paradoxes. Un-whatever marketing can help you create your own paradox.

Why Does It Work?

- **Unique.** It requires you to differentiate yourself in a completely opposite way (as opposed to slightly), which will automatically set you apart if you are able to achieve it.
- **Authentic.** In a case where competitors have lost their connections and you are offering something different, you have the chance to become the authentic choice.
- **Talkable.** Being an opposing factor through un-whatever marketing means that you will be part of conversations where the ordinary alternative is discussed.

WHEN SHOULD YOU USE IT?

Green Light: When It Works	Red Light: When to Avoid It
This works best when you are in a crowded market with many competitors and you are not the market leader. In that case you can authentically stand for something different and position yourself as the un-whatever in a believable way.	The most common situation in which you may need to avoid this approach is if your product or service is very marginally different from the rest of the pack. This won't work if your actual product or service doesn't measure up.

Who's Doing It?

1. **7UP.** Back in the 1960s, 7UP embarked on a groundbreaking marketing campaign in which the noncaffeinated soft drink was described as the "uncola." A series of popular television ads featuring actor Geoffrey Holder showed him holding a kola nut in one hand and an "uncola nut" (lemon or lime) in the other. The ads successfully positioned 7UP as the soft drink to have when you didn't want a Coke or Pepsi. Over time, the drink lost its status as multiple competitors flooded the market; however, the idea of positioning the drink at the time to stand apart from the most recognized cola players was a strategic move that got people to notice it.

2. **Virgin Anything.** As we discussed in Chapter 3, Virgin is a master brand at tackling staid industries and positioning its brand as the un-whatever. Whether it is credit cards, airlines, sodas, or wedding dresses, a core part of Virgin's strategy when entering any industry is understanding the conventions of the industry, and finding smart ways to break them. As Sir Richard Branson himself is fond of retelling, the reason he first entered the airline industry is that he had a subpar experience and thought to himself that he could do better. Virgin's philosophy ever since (though it may not always work), has been to break conventions in an industry and stand at the opposite end of the pole from its competitors. Extreme differentiation of your product or service is where un-whatever marketing works.

3. **Taco Bell.** The un-whatever marketing technique is also quite common when it comes to the food industry. Taco Bell also found their un-whatever through their brilliant tagline encouraging their consumers to "think outside the bun." With it, they successfully defined fast food as being more than just hamburgers and fries, and also found their own niche among the growing number of vegetarians who previously had few meal options at fast food restaurants.

Un-Whatever Marketing, Step by Step

1. **Define the "whatever."** An essential part of using un-whatever marketing is to build a clear picture of what you want the "whatever" to be. This does not necessarily need to be a particular competitor, but rather can be a type of business that typifies an industry. The best way to start is usually to create a list of competitors and make a list of the qualities, policies, and messages

they all share. Then you can try to spot common threads and identify areas where you can differ.

2. **Make sure your position is compelling.** This technique won't work if your angle is less appealing than the opposing version you are trying to differentiate from. The points you differ on must be things that people care about or see as important.

3. **Target the disgruntled.** When you are using an un-whatever marketing technique, the best way to promote it is by targeting those that are disgruntled with everything else out there. Finding them, today, is similar to the idea of finding accidental spokespeople, which was covered in Chapter 2. They are often vocal and they share their thoughts online, so you can find them fairly easily.

4. **Gruntle them.** You probably won't believe this, but "gruntle" is really a word. It means "to put in good humor," and it is a fitting description for what you really want to do with your customers. The best moments in which to use the un-whatever marketing technique can be in industries where nearly every option a consumer has is subpar in some way and where you can stand alone for giving customers what they have been asking or waiting for.

Sensory Marketing

What Is It?

Sensory marketing is about having marketing messages that go beyond sight and sound. A sensory experience is one that uses the other senses, including smell, touch, and taste. Some of the senses may seem like fairly obvious fits. Of course a restaurant is going to use taste, and a fabric store will likely use touch. These are easy examples of sensory marketing.

It is the other unexpected uses that make this a more interesting technique to consider. Using the sense of touch to market a book or the sense of smell to build interest in a car are good examples of this.

Why Does It Work?

- **Unique.** The essence of sensory marketing is to focus on the senses that no one else is targeting. As a result, you can stand out.
- **Authentic.** Sensory experiences are real, and are difficult to fake. Something either smells nice, or it doesn't, which means the experience is usually authentic.
- **Talkable.** People learn and remember in different ways. By using other senses, you can create an experience that many of your customers will remember and share because it was unexpected.

WHEN SHOULD YOU USE IT?

Green Light: When It Works	Red Light: When to Avoid It
When most of your competitors are focused on the obvious sensory experiences for your product or industry, offering an unexpected experience stands out.	Since a sensory experience is a physical thing, it is limited by physical constraints as well. Smell, for example, is a tough sense to use for an online retailer.

Who's Doing It?

1. **Ford's doors.** In 2006, the J.D. Power & Associates initial quality study on new cars started including the sound that a car door makes as a factor in their overall quality assessment. In an interview with *BusinessWeek* magazine, J.D. Power executive director Joe Ivers noted that "the door closure and chime is the car's second impression after exterior design." It's the reason why Ford's global chief of product development, Derrick M. Kuzak, decided that for the new 2008 models of the Ford Taurus and the Ford Flex, the sound the door makes when it closes was going to be a critical design factor. The result, after extensive product testing, was a new system that created a "vaultlike" sound when the door closes on the Taurus. By focusing on the sensory experience, Ford successfully demonstrated the trustworthiness and safety of their new cars through a sonic experience as well as a

physical one. It has already paid off, as the Ford Taurus earned a five-star safety rating from NHTSA and is being promoted as the "safest full-size car in America."

2. **Hoopla.** A book titled *Hoopla* features a collection of creative work produced by the ad agency Crispin Porter & Bogusky. The book's jacket feels like sandpaper, and the back cover shares a tongue-in-cheek story about how the cover was intentionally done in an abrasive way—to "harvest DNA" through skin cells so the book would serve a dual purpose as a source of ideas as well as a DNA collection device for eventual cloning. The cover uses a sensory experience to demonstrate the personality behind the book: unconventional, quirky, and creative. This is a common technique in book jacket design (though not to the extreme that *Hoopla* uses it). The power of tactile response is a key factor in using matte or glossy (versus soft) finishes for book covers.

3. **Tropicana Pure.** Early in 2008, Tropicana relaunched their premium brand called Tropicana Pure by describing it as a sensory experience that went beyond just the taste of the juice. It was the texture, the smell, the look all together that made it stand out. It may seem strange to talk about senses beyond taste or smell when you're just marketing orange juice, but when the brand asked some of the early product testers about the juice, it received the same feedback from all of them. The juice really did provide a sensory experience, and was something that lived up to the sensory promise.

4. **The Messengers' secret ringtone.** When Sony Pictures started promoting its teen-targeted horror flick *The Messengers* in early 2007, Sony needed a unique hook that would also get teens talking about the film. To create it, the company launched a viral

campaign whereby teens could download ringtones online that would be audible only to them and not to adults—taking advantage of the ability of young people to hear a higher frequency of sound than older adults. Offering this sound on a ringtone that tied into the movie provided a sensory experience that teens could share privately, and that adults were excluded from. It was a brilliant use of sensory marketing to drive engagement in an upcoming film that hinged on getting teenagers talking to one another in an environment without parents.

Sensory Marketing, Step by Step

1. **Uncover the hidden senses.** Every business inherently markets to a certain sense. Food markets to taste. Music markets to hearing. Most everything markets to your sense of sight. The first thing you need to do is figure out which senses are key to your business and are the ones that you usually market to. Those are the expected senses. Now make a list of the senses that are not on the list. With only five senses, this shouldn't take you too long.

2. **Get creative about using them.** Now that you have uncovered the hidden senses, you are ready to start creating a way to use them (as well as the expected senses). Sensory marketing needs to have a creative idea. Simply telling people to experience your product or service in an unexpected way is not enough. You need to have an idea for how to do it.

3. **Make it strategic.** The challenge of getting creative is to make it strategic. Imagine sending mints along with a book to get someone to think "fresh" about the concepts in the book. It doesn't seem like an inspiring idea, yet when I got a preview copy of

a book called *Fire Them Up* by Carmine Gallo in 2007, it came with a box of red hot candies. It was a great sensory fit for a book that was all about creating a fire among your employees.

4. **Encourage sharing.** The nice thing about sensory marketing is that it offers an experience rather than something for someone to read and digest. As a result, it can become a very shareable experience that travels easily from person to person. The ultimate goal of creating your sensory experience and using this technique of marketing should be to give people something they can pass along to others.

Antimarketer Marketing

What Is It?

There is a reason why many people have a low opinion of marketing. At its worst, it is interruptive, annoying, badly timed, irrelevant, and stupid. We all know this type of marketing too well—and usually do our best to avoid it. The problem is, for every great marketing message, there seem to be 10 others that are amateur efforts, blatantly overstating product benefits, and presuming an audience of idiots. These are the marketing messages that are always ignored, and that give the entire field of marketing a bad reputation. I want *PNI* to help you make sure that your marketing messages do not fall into this category.

The power of antimarketer marketing is that it offers you a way to stand beside your customers and shake your head at all the other clueless marketers that approach them in the traditional way. It puts you at the dinner table alongside your customers when that annoying telemarketer calls. More important, you have the chance to rise above them because you are essentially saying to your customers that you have abandoned that type of marketing and are therefore more trustworthy than those who practice it. It also requires a sense of humor about the usual marketing that your customers may be used to.

Why Does It Work?

- **Unique.** Using this technique puts you in a position of sympathizing with your customers, who are being bombarded with marketing messages from everyone else. It sets you apart.
- **Authentic.** By siding with the customers and poking fun at "traditional" marketing, you demonstrate to your customers that you don't think that method is right, and that you want to treat them more authentically.

- **Talkable.** The idea of anyone making fun of this aspect of your business (including the way you used to do business) can, if done right, create a memorable impression, and one that people will tell others about.

WHEN SHOULD YOU USE IT?

Green Light: When It Works	Red Light: When to Avoid It
Use this technique when there are a large number of marketers in your industry who are using interruption as a marketing tactic to try to get your customers' attention.	If your previous marketing efforts for the brand are of the same type that you now are trying to denounce, you need to have a good story of rehabilitation or risk being outed for being hypocritical.

Who's Doing It?

1. **Axe.** The Axe brand has been built through unconventional marketing. Breaking out of the deodorant category and positioning its products as a "body spray," the Axe brand stands for sex, and promises guys who wear it that girls will be unable to resist them. Are guys really dumb enough to believe that the body spray has this effect on women, like a bottled pheromone? (Okay, the answer to that question probably depends on your gender.) Regardless, the marketing paints an irresistible picture and tells guys that how they smell matters to women, and that a simple deodorant under the arm isn't enough. You need a full body spray. So for

an irreverent product like this, using an antimarketer marketing strategy is key. A recent Axe campaign video features Axe making fun of its own marketing (and marketing in general). The end result is that Axe continues to break out of its own category.

2. **30Rock.** A popular sitcom currently on television called *30Rock* has been winning awards and breaking conventions in comedy by making fun of the one group that is usually untouchable: the network studios. The show is on NBC, is set in the NBC-Universal building, and follows the humorous adventures of a group of writers and producers of a sketch-comedy show. It is a comedic behind-the-scenes look at how TV shows are produced, but what sets it apart is how it manages to integrate product placements and branded messages into the show in a completely over-the-top way. Every brand is mentioned in oddly inappropriate situations that are obviously inserted for the product to be part of the show. At times, the actors even look at the camera after doing the product placement and ask if they can get paid yet. The show's format makes fun of marketing while marketing at the same time. As a result, the product placement messages stand out even more and become noticeable.

Antimarketer Marketing, Step by Step

1. **Map the competition.** In order to effectively use the antimarketer marketing technique, you first need to understand what the traits of the common marketer are in your business or industry. The best way to do that is to put together a list of your key competitors (both real and the ones that you would aspire to compete with), and then note the common traits or styles of marketing they choose. Do they all focus on product features? Are

they all offering some type of discount to drive purchases? Knowing these common elements is the first step in countering them.

2. **Find the pain points.** The most successful examples of anti-marketer marketing happen when the current marketing that people are experiencing is somehow painful. The power of this technique is that it puts you on the side of your customers. If you can avoid causing your customer an inconvenience through your message, you are already on the right track.

3. **Use the "but."** To paint the full picture of how you are different from other marketers, you need to first demonstrate what others are doing. Setting your message up this way introduces a common experience and allows you to say "but" before telling your own story. For example: "We could tell you about the eight autonomic megapixels and decompressed ventriloquistic Carl Zeiss lens on our new digital cameras, BUT all you really care about is that your daughter won't be blurry when you photograph her at her big game."

4. **Have a bonding moment.** Visually, this is the moment when the actor looks directly at you, winks, and tells you something not as an actor but as a person. This same bonding moment happens in print and in direct one-on-one conversations. Essentially, the bonding moment occurs when the communicator "breaks character" from marketing and delivers his or her anti-marketing message.

5. **Don't apologize.** The antimarketer marketing message is the one that you don't need to apologize for. It has power because instead of pretending that you are not marketing, you are entirely up-front about it, and in fact you make fun of other marketers for not admitting it.

Fallibility Marketing

What Is It?

Nothing offers the ability to show your humanity quite like screwing up. Real people make mistakes and have to own up to them, yet companies have traditionally done this very poorly. The typical faceless corporation will admit no wrongdoing, refuse to apologize, and offer compensation that is woefully inadequate for whatever it has done wrong. To a degree, you could consider the moments when a company fails in some way or lets its customers down to be ultimate personality moments.

Fallibility marketing is about taking those moments when you make a mistake or something goes wrong and turning them into an opportunity to build an even stronger relationship with your customer. To do this you need to be able to recognize the problem and offer a solution, or point to a solution that is in progress. You also need to be sure that it is not a consistent problem. Fallibility marketing will never work if you are always making mistakes or screwing up all the time. It cannot save a bad product or substandard service.

Why Does It Work?

- **Unique.** Companies that solve problems immediately and are able to admit they have a problem are unexpected and welcomed.
- **Authentic.** Using your weak moments as a chance to open a dialogue with your customers can create a lasting connection more powerful than you would have if you never made any mistakes.
- **Talkable.** There is no more talkable story than one of a customer who had something go wrong and then had it immediately and properly fixed by employees at a company that truly cared about making it right.

WHEN SHOULD YOU USE IT?

Green Light: When It Works	Red Light: When to Avoid It
If your mistakes or problems are out of the ordinary, and you are able to offer a resolution relatively quickly, this type of marketing can be ideal.	When you screw up over and over, this type of marketing will never work. Your issues need to be solvable and infrequent.

Who's Doing It?

1. **Most "Web 2.0" sites.** The "404 error page" is thankfully dying across newer Web sites. These nondescriptive error pages were once all over the Web as a standard way of telling you that a "file is not found." These faceless pages of the Internet are a perfect example of the way not to screw up. Web 2.0 sites, on the other hand, have for the most part managed to replace these faceless pages with more personable messages. Digg.com, for example, shows a page with a list of favorite other sites from its development team any time the site is down. This page essentially invites you to visit a few other great sites while you are waiting for Digg to be back up, and promises to be back up soon. Other sites feature well-designed pages helping you get to the content you may be looking for, take you to the site search, or redirect you from old pages (which may still be bookmarked as broken links) to new associated pages. Someday soon, it is likely, the nondescriptive 404 error page will be a relic of the past.

2. **Southwest Airlines.** Seeing an airline brand as an example of how to use your mistakes may seem ironic, considering that airlines' mistakes are plentiful and relatively consistent. At Southwest, however, these mistakes are treated as opportunities to build customer loyalty. The brand has a group of individuals dedicated to a more proactive style of customer service; it spots mistakes and lapses, apologizes for them, and tries to compensate customers accordingly. Many customers share stories of situations in which they were forced to deal with extreme delays, and apologized to by the airline and even compensated with free tickets. It is no wonder that amid the many bankruptcies and financial woes in the U.S. airline industry, Southwest has managed to weather the storm and continues to remain profitable. In part, this is because the airline treats its mistakes as an opportunity to excel, which few of its competitors do.

Fallibility Marketing, Step by Step

1. **Actively listen.** The only way you can engage in fallibility marketing is by first realizing the mistakes that you are making. Doing that involves not just listening to what your customers are telling you directly (that is obvious), but also listening to what they are publicly telling others outside of their interactions with you. This means actively listening to conversations happening online and in personal interactions between your employees and people in the real world.

2. **Acknowledge the problem.** This seems obvious, but doing it gets you past the barrier of belief. If a customer is dissatisfied, it doesn't mean he or she is right, but the feeling is valid. Figuring out who is right and who is wrong is the first thing to leave

behind. Simply acknowledge that the customer feels like something was not right.

3. **Demonstrate that you care.** An element similar to acknowledging the problem is finding a way to show that it matters to you personally. This is the moment when authentic behavior shines, so be sure you can find a way to really care.

4. **Offer an apology.** Apologies go a long way, and are a necessary part of fallibility marketing. If you are going to use your screwup as an opportunity, you need to do more than acknowledge that there was a screwup and care about it. You need to offer a real apology. This gets you past the inevitable comment that every bad situation generates, which is a customer saying that everything could have been better if you had just apologized. Even if it doesn't seem like it would matter, it does.

5. **Try to fix it.** This is likely not a news flash for you, but offering an apology won't do much if you are unable to actually fix the problem, so do everything humanly possible to try. Resolution is key.

6. **Don't screw the same thing up again.** The final point is that you can't repeat the same mistakes a second time, or you will lose credibility.

Insider Marketing

What Is It?

There is a scene in the James Bond film *Die Another Day* where Bond, fresh from escaping from the bad guys, walks into a five-star hotel in rags. The front staff recognize him immediately, welcome him back to the hotel, give him his "regular room," and send up his favorite bubbly (a bottle of '61 Bollinger). Bond is the ultimate VIP, and the way he is treated is what every one of your customers wants. The power of feeling like a VIP is about being an insider. When you have exclusive access that few others have, you are special. Insider marketing is about creating this feeling, either with a physical destination, or with information that is not widely distributed.

Why Does It Work?

- **Unique.** It makes your customers feel important and trusted.
- **Authentic.** It raises the chances that the customers will respond to it as it is not a "mass" message.
- **Talkable.** It is inherently talkable, as people love to share stories of special treatment or access with others.

WHEN SHOULD YOU USE IT?

Green Light: When It Works	Red Light: When to Avoid It
This technique works best when you have something exclusive to share and can limit access to it. It is also ideal for the type of business that relies on repeat customers to build its brand.	If the exclusivity is not believable or too widespread to actually be considered exclusive, this technique will not work. The exclusive information or access must also be significant and not ordinary.

Who's Doing It?

1. **Gmail launch.** Google's now frequently copied launch strategy for Gmail in 2004 is one of the best examples of how insider marketing can work. The only way you could get a Gmail account was to be invited by someone who already had a Gmail account. For some time, getting a Gmail account was the ultimate symbol of geek cool, even causing some people to bid several hundred dollars on eBay for invites from people so that they could create their own accounts even if they didn't know anyone who could invite them.

2. **The Gambler's Special.** One of the tips that experienced travelers to Las Vegas love to share is what many consider the best deal for a meal on the Strip. At Mr. Lucky's restaurant in the Hard Rock Café in Vegas, there is a hidden menu item called the Gambler's Special. For $7.77 you get a steak, three shrimp, and your choice of a potato or broccoli. It is served 24 hours a

day, seven days a week, but you need to ask for it by name. It is the ultimate insider deal in a town full of exclusive access and VIP lounges. Most of them require you to spend (or lose) lots of money to become a VIP. At the Hard Rock Café Las Vegas, all you need to do is know is what to ask for.

3. **The Konami Code.** Video games have taken the art of insider access to a new level. Many games now feature hidden levels, secret hacks, and other unknown elements that people pass on to one another by word of mouth. One of the most famous is symbolized by a sequence that many old Nintendo enthusiasts will recognize: "Up-up-down-down-left-right-left-right-B-A-Start." Known as the Konami Code, this string was a secret hack hidden in multiple video games created by the Konami company that would allow you to power up with multiple lives. Made popular specifically in a game called Contra, the secret code would give you 30 lives instead of the usual 3, allowing you to successfully make it through the game to victory. The line today is a classic retro cult hit, even inspiring a band who call themselves this and tour around the United States (search MySpace and you can see their profile!).

4. **Most musicians and artists.** Nearly all musicians and artists, no matter how small their fan base, have already figured out insider marketing. They tell their fans before anyone else knows about shows, album releases, and more, letting them have exclusive access, confident that the fans will tell lots of other people. Surprisingly few businesses of any size have as great an awareness of this strategy. Musicians and artists are not marketing geniuses—they are just using a technique that works because people love to feel like VIPs. It would work for you too.

Insider Marketing, Step by Step

1. **Nominate your insiders.** The first step for using an insider marketing strategy is to find the right people to target. There are essentially three ways to target the right audience to use this technique.

   a. *Action based.* Insiders are in this group based on some activity that they have performed. This could be filling out a form or survey, attending an event, purchasing a particular product, or some other action taken by a customer.

   b. *Qualifier based.* This is the most common method for targeting; it involves a certain predictable qualifier, such as frequency of travel (for airlines), amount spent (for retail), or referrals (for multilevel marketing—such as the method used by Avon or SeaSilver).

   c. *Invitation based.* This last method for targeting includes all other methods, because invitations to be part of an exclusive club can be based on anything, from personal relationships to reputation.

2. **Offer them something exclusive.** Once you have the right people targeted, you actually need to offer them something that is just for insiders. The amount of loyalty an insider marketing program can generate is usually directly proportional to the value of what you are able to offer them.

3. **Keep it exclusive.** Nothing will kill an insider marketing program faster than opening the insider access up to anyone who wants it. This will not only cheapen the experience for everyone, but will likely cause backlash from the first entrants into the program who may subsequently feel like they were tricked into joining something that no longer offers benefit or values their loyalty.

4. **Make the experience repeatable.** A key element of real VIP

treatment, as the James Bond example illustrates, is that it is repeatable and not a one-time experience. Insider marketing requires consistent special treatment, either through physical interactions or through information and content that is shared. Once you make people insiders, you need to find ways to keep them feeling like they still are.

Useful Marketing

What Is It?

This may be one of the most straightforward marketing techniques, but it is routinely ignored or forgotten about. Useful marketing is all about content. Creating content with value and then letting people find and use it remains a great way to demonstrate that your brand is about more than just profits.

Why Does It Work?

- **Unique.** The best content is something that offers insight and value and cannot be found elsewhere.
- **Authentic.** It proves that you are not just focused on marketing and selling a product.
- **Talkable.** Useful content is the one type of information that people will automatically share with others.

WHEN SHOULD YOU USE IT?

Green Light: When It Works	Red Light: When to Avoid It
Creating content that is useful for your customers can work in most situations, regardless of what you are selling.	Don't use this technique if you cannot create unbiased and useful content, or keep it up-to-date on a consistent basis.

1. **Weber Nation.** Weber Grills first started more than 50 years ago as the result of a wildly popular new dome-shaped grill designed by a metalworker in Illinois who was frustrated by the grills available at the time and experimented with a new method. George Stephen's invention, called George's Barbecue Kettle, became a local phenomenon in the Midwest in the 1960s and has spread nationally and internationally since then. Today, Weber is considered by most avid grillers as the top brand. The interesting thing about it, however, is that a key element of the company's growth is not just the creation of a great and beloved product, but also its ability to maintain a steadfast focus on sharing useful content with its customers. In addition to its grilling products, it publishes cookbooks featuring grilling recipes and lessons on how to grill. The company also provides downloadable PDFs online that talk not only about its products, but about how to select a gas grill and what to look for. Most significant, it has created a robust online community called Weber Nation, which it describes as "the site for real people who love their Weber Grills." You could argue that Weber's great products are the reason for the company's success; however, it is the continual focus on education and creating useful tools, downloads, and content that adds significantly to the reason why Weber Nation is so popular.

2. **Widgets.** This is not a specific company, but rather an entire trend that is getting a lot of attention today. Essentially, widgets are small pieces of online content that organizations can offer for download or integrate into existing social networks to provide some type of functionality. TripAdvisor, a travel review site, has a popular widget that allows you to create a list of all the cities

you have visited in the world. Apple's operating system allows you to download widgets for everything from the weather to stock quotes. Many other groups offer downloadable programs that sit on your desktop and provide a variety of useful features. The point is, widget marketing allows you to create something useful, makes it portable for your customers, and then lets them interact with it on an ongoing basis.

Useful Marketing, Step by Step

1. **Focus on the decision-making process first.** Most useful marketing somehow factors into your customers' decision-making process. This means creating useful tips for what to look for in particular products, ideas on how to use a service, and thoughts about an entire industry that may be relevant. The aim of useful marketing should be to get your content in front of a customer at the right point in her or his decision-making process.

2. **Don't be afraid of the competitors.** Useful marketing will never work if you are afraid to go head-to-head with your competitors. The most useful content is not biased or willing to offer multiple solutions. This does not mean, however, that you need to focus on every element of a purchase decision. If there are some that you win on and some that you lose, focus on those you can win (but make sure the content is still useful).

3. **Demonstrate thinking rather than features.** Remember, being useful is not about pushing a sales message. It is about creating something relevant that people will likely want to save, print, or at least keep track of in case they need it in the future.

4. **Encourage dialogue and respond to it.** In many cases, your creating useful content may solicit some follow-up questions from

your customers about what you meant. Answering these questions fairly and openly is a core element of using this technique of marketing.

5. **Make it easy to share.** The truth about useful content is that the more useful it is, the more your customers will likely want to share it with others. To that end, if you can make it easy to share, either physically or online, it will help your message to travel further without creating artificial barriers.

Incidental Marketing

What Is It?

The fact that I am Indian is probably incidental for any of you who have bought this book. If you bought it, you probably did so for the ideas inside of it, or because of the cover, or perhaps because you had heard about it from someone. Regardless of the reason, my ethnicity is not likely to be a big factor in selling this book. Yet if I were to promote the book based on being Indian, in certain communities, that would be an example of incidental marketing.

This is not so uncommon if you think about it. Have you ever sat in a job interview where the interviewer looked at your credentials and saw that although you were qualified, it was your interest in Greek archaeology, or your world championship title in Scrabble that really piqued her interest? These incidental elements are hooks that can sometimes help to create a connection. This is the same idea that you can explore for your marketing.

Why Does It Work?

- **Unique.** Incidental points are highly individual and offer insight into an unexpected element of your character or the character of your organization.
- **Authentic.** The only way that this technique is truly useful is when it presents something that is true and incidental.
- **Talkable.** Often the incidental elements of a story are the most interesting and therefore talkable.

WHEN SHOULD YOU USE IT?

Green Light: When It Works	Red Light: When to Avoid It
This can work when you can find a true element of your brand and/or service to promote	Avoid this when an incidental point cannot be fabricated and needs to still have some element of relevance.

Who's Doing It?

1. **The Haka.** The All Blacks is one of the best rugby teams in the world. The team has won global championships, is a feared adversary, and derives its name from the color of its uniforms (all black, of course). On the surface the team seems like any other, featuring an arsenal of guys with thick necks and tough exteriors. Yet the incidental aspect of this team is that it is from New Zealand. In a world where most indigenous cultures have been nearly wiped out, the predominance of the Maori culture in New Zealand is a notable contradiction, as anyone who has traveled to the island will tell you. What makes the All Blacks stand out beyond being a good rugby team is a tradition that stems from the Maori culture of New Zealand. Before every game, the entire team lines up to face its opponent and does a war dance called the Haka. If the idea of a full team doing a dance in front of its opponents before a match seems a bit juvenile, watching the Haka just once will quickly rid you of that view. It is a fierce, chest-slapping, loud, and intimidating dance. Imag-

ine yourself as the opponent, and you can see the psychological power that the Haka offers to the team. It is the reason why most rugby fans (no matter what their allegiance) consider seeing a game with the All Blacks playing to be the ultimate fan experience. Being from New Zealand may be incidental, but it is the most significant element of the team's personality and a large part of the reason it gathers such a large international following of fans.

2. **Free prizes.** Let's face it, free prizes are usually worthless. Consider breakfast cereal companies, which are the worst offenders when it comes to freebies. Every few weeks a new product makes its way inside a cereal box, and often it is what creates the necessity for buying the box. This is not just a strategy aimed at kids; adults are equally targeted with their own special offers. Cracker Jacks box are just overly sweetened popcorn with nuts, yet the free prize inside a Cracker Jack box offers a nostalgic moment that is almost irresistible. As a result, it is another marketing example of how something incidental can be the factor that helps to drive purchases.

Incidental Marketing, Step by Step

1. **Think outside the law.** A good place to begin thinking about the incidental attributes of your brand that you may be able to use is to consider those things that you are not legally allowed to promote. This means race, ethnicity, gender, age, disability, or location, to name a few. This may seem like strange advice, but many times these elements can be assets for a brand if used as part of a smart incidental marketing strategy.

2. **Get over the resistance.** The first thought you will likely have about this strategy is that it seems irrelevant or perhaps opportunistic. Sometimes good ideas require you to think a bit differently. If you think about it, you will agree that this is not so uncommon. If you have ever responded to government or corporate RFPs, you know that sometimes they have provisions that require certain conditions, for example, that 50 percent of the contracts awarded for a certain project must go to female-owned businesses. This is an example of the government mandating you to use incidental marketing. Does this qualification really have any bearing on a company's ability to do the job? Probably not, but it is used as a qualifier nonetheless.

3. **Communicate the incidental message to the right niche.** The way to maximize the effectiveness of an incidental element of your business is to target a particular niche audience with it, probably the same audience that aligns itself with your incidental attribute. This group will in most cases offer the strongest targeting opportunity for your message.

4. **Keep it incidental.** The power of this style of marketing is also best utilized if you do not let it overtake your entire marketing strategy. This is a niche strategy useful for reaching a particular segment of your customers; however, it should not replace your more comprehensive strategy. If it does, that's a sign that what you are doing is not actually focusing on something incidental.

GUIDES & TOOLS

Taking Theory Further

A recent IBM series of TV ads implores business professionals to "Stop Talking. Start Doing." That's where we are now in *PNI*. It's time to stop talking about the power of personality and really get down to the logistics of doing. In this section, you will. To do this, I have outlined the Guides and Tools by Chapter for easy reference from Part One to Part Two.

MASTER LIST OF GUIDES & TOOLS BY CHAPTER

CHAPTER 1
 	
Being faceless no longer works
	Are you faceless? The Quick Six-Point Test
	How to:
	    make your brand more likeable
	    rethink the small print

CHAPTER 2
 	
Accidental Spokespeople
	A Spokesperson Comparison Model
	How to:
	    empower your employees
	    create a successful corporate blog
	    hire the right employees with personality

CHAPTER 3 **UAT Filter**	Deconstructing Personality: An Outline The UAT Filter: Quick Reference Chart

Chapter 1 Guides & Tools

Are You Faceless? The Quick Six-Point Test

Directions

1. Answer these six questions truthfully about your business.

2. Start to ask these questions internally.

3. If you don't get a perfect score (6 yes answers), use the other guides to do something about it.

THE TEST

The World's Greatest Test to Find Out If You Are Faceless

	YES	NO
Individuality: Is there a real individual or group of individuals that your customers associate by name as the people behind your organization? (Fictional characters or personas don't count.)	☐	☐
Backstory: Does your organization have a credible history (backstory) that consumers can understand, connect with, and talk about?	☐	☐
Relationships: Do you have a way to recognize your repeat customers by face, name, or voice so that they are not treated like new customers each time they contact you?	☐	☐

	YES	NO
Policies: Can individual employees choose to change or bend policies based on their interactions with customers?	❏	❏
Language: If you read your marketing, sales, or Web site descriptions for your business out loud, does it sound like a real person is saying it?	❏	❏
Spokespeople: Are individual employees encouraged to tell their friends, families, and contacts about what they do, and are they given training in how the company describes and positions itself?	❏	❏

There are only two possible ways to score on this test.

1. **Perfect Score (6 yes answers)**

   Congratulations! If you have a perfect score on the facelessness test, that means you are already ahead of most companies and well on your way to using personality effectively to differentiate your business and connect with your customers. The real challenge for you is to make sure you are taking advantage of all your personality moments. In every business, there will be moments when you have your customers' attention but are not using it in the best way possible to meet their needs and demonstrate the essence of your brand. Your priority should be to try to get even better at spotting these moments and use them more effectively.

2. **Not a Perfect Score (anything less than 6 yes answers)**

   If you scored less than a 6, don't worry, you have plenty of company. You might be wondering why there isn't a sliding scale on this test. It's not that I'm not giving you credit for getting some yeses. Every response you could truthfully make with a yes is good news. Yet there is still room to make some changes to give your brand more personality. The guides and tools in this section as well as the lessons shared earlier in the book will help you improve on this score.

How to Make Your Brand More Likeable

1. **Change your hiring priorities.**

   Most people tend to hire employees whom they like and can associate with, but do this mainly for roles that they consider "customer facing." This is not enough. As we have seen throughout the book, anyone can become an accidental spokesperson for your brand, even people who were not originally hired for roles in which they were intended to be in front of your customers. If you can make likeability a hiring priority for any member of your team, regardless of how much interaction he or she is meant to have with a customer, you will be on your way to increasing the likeability of your brand.

2. **Stop punishing your customers.**

   The people working in your company are only part of the story. Likeability also means forgiving customers for small mistakes and making sure that your policies and method of doing business are not set up to penalize them needlessly. If a customer brings back a product to your store 32 days after she or he bought it (missing the typical 30-day window), accept the return. If someone buys something from you for $6.03 and doesn't have three cents, tell the customer not to worry about it. If there is a procedure costing thousands of dollars at your clinic, don't force patients to pay $3.00 for parking. These are the little things that customers pay attention to, and the ones that make the difference between likeable brands and brands that people simply put up with because they must.

3. Let them see your individuality.

A key element of likeability is that you need to have more individuals in your company and fewer "people." Individuals offer a personal connection that demonstrates that your organization is not just a big entity, but is made up of a collection of unique and authentic personalities. If you have managed to change your hiring priorities, then these individuals will each be likeable enough that they can build that same foundation for your brand.

4. Listen more.

This is an old tenet of customer service, but it is still true. If a customer feels listened to and respected, no matter what the situation, he or she will rate your organization and people as more likeable. There are many ways to respond to this fact. The first and most obvious is to listen to what your customers are telling you directly—either in person, on the phone, or online. The next is to also monitor conversations online that may already be happening. The third is something I recommended earlier: active listening. This means more than just listening or monitoring, but actually engaging in a dialogue with customers. Online, this may involve commenting on blogs, participating in online communities, or posting answers to questions online. Offline, this could include being a part of relevant events, and collecting feedback and experiences from employees.

5. **Do favors instead of expecting them.**

   Doing a favor for a customer is not the same thing as offering a discount. Discounts or other sales promotions are self-serving, whereas favors are done based on a belief. When you ask your customers to tell a friend about your company, you are asking them for a favor. There may be an incentive for them behind it, but the favor is in the asking. But before you can be in a position to ask for these favors, you need to be providing them to your customers first. This is related to the technique of Karmic marketing discussed on page 196.

How to Rethink Your Small Print

1. **Don't try to hide it.**

   Small print is the enemy of most consumers. It signifies the "catch" in any offer, and the things that companies don't want you to read. The main problem with the small print is that it creates an atmosphere of distrust and makes customers suspect that you are hiding the truth from them. Therefore, you need to stop trying to hide any small print that may exist in your written communications. This may be a visual or a design choice in your online or offline advertisements, contracts, or warranties. The less you focus on what your customers won't get, the more you can focus on what they will.

2. Think like a copywriter.

Another problem with small print and legal disclaimers is that they sometimes seem to go on forever. In the world of copywriting, and particularly in advertising, word choice matters. Taglines are designed to be minimalistic. Nike's "Just do it" still stands as a memorable summation of the brand in part because it is so simple. If marketers were charged by the word for their disclaimers, these would quickly get a lot shorter. The simplest way to rethink your small print is in terms of number of words. Make it a priority to use fewer of them.

3. Make your lawyer work harder.

In order to use fewer words, you are going to have to make your lawyer do something few organizations ever really do: demand more humanity. The truth about most legal disclaimers and other forms of small print is that they are so long because they are standardized. You wouldn't buy advertising copy to promote your business in the form of standardized templates, yet that is exactly what many businesses, large and small, do when it comes to legal language. Finding a good lawyer who has a mastery of phrasing is a key element in rethinking your small print, because it will get you past the cutting and pasting job that many less hardworking lawyers are ready to pawn off on unsuspecting businesses as mandatory language.

4. Inject humor appropriately.

In the Introduction, we saw the power of using humor in a disclaimer for Apple. The reason that humor can make such a powerful statement is that small print is really the last place that any consumer expects to see it. Did you notice the unique small print on the copyright page of this book? This is not to say you should turn your legal disclaimers into joke collections, or dilute the substance of your messages. There are few lawyers who would go for that, anyway. But finding an appropriate opportunity to include humor can go a long way toward putting your customers at ease.

Chapter 2 Guides & Tools

How to Embrace Your Accidental Spokespeople

1. **Find them.**

    The first step in learning how to embrace your accidental spokes-people is to find them. There are several methods for doing this—regardless of whether you are looking at employees, partners, or customers. These are:

    - **Surveying**—This method involves creating some sort of survey that you can distribute to your employees, partners, or customers, asking them questions designed to bring out the accidental spokespeople among them. Questions could include whether or not they have a blog, how often they tend to talk about your company or products to friends and family, whether they see themselves as an advocate for purchasing behavior from their network, and similar questions.

    - **Searching**—As it sounds, this method involves conducting online searches through a combination of traditional search engines and blog search engines, and perhaps contracting with a company who has software available to help you search online conversations more easily.

    - **Referrals**—Asking your customers or partners how they heard about you is a perfect way to spot the accidental spokespeople who may not have become apparent through searching. If the name of someone or of a particular Web site comes up fairly often as a source driving new customers or partners in your direction, you may want to add that person to your list of accidental spokespeople.

- **Listening**—There are many situations in which you will be interacting with your customers and partners and they will offer clues about how vocal to be about your business or products. Keeping track of these clues will also allow you to find the emerging accidental spokespeople you may want to pay attention to.

2. **Make it easy for them to find you.**

Making it easy for your accidental spokespeople to let you know who they are may be something as simple as posting a form on a Web site asking your customers if they are blogging about you and requesting them to send you the URL. It could also be a part of existing loyalty programs as long as the point is to separate simple enthusiasts (people who like and buy your product) from accidental spokespeople (enthusiasts who are vocally telling others about your product online or offline).

3. **Open a dialogue with them.**

Once you know who your accidental spokespeople are, it is important to determine what type of relationship you can have with them. Whether the individuals you uncovered are enthusiasts or detractors, creating a dialogue is an important step. It not only lets them know that you are listening, but for detractors it tells them that you are aware of their unhappiness and want to reverse it. For enthusiasts, it can be a great ego boost for them to know that you are listening and that their enthusiasm matters to you. This dialogue puts you in a position that allows you to respond to their requests or suggestions and learn from them.

4. **Help them collaborate with each other.**

Very often, your best accidental spokespeople are sharing their opinions out of passion but not necessarily linked to one another. One of the smartest things you can do for them is to find ways to help them collaborate. This may mean hosting events, or simply putting them in contact with one another. Introducing two people who are enthusiasts for your brand or products will lead to good things.

5. **Treat them like insiders (take them seriously).**

The worst thing you can do once you have built relationships with your accidental spokespeople is to exclude them from important new announcements or happenings in your business, or do something they would be interested in without involving them. Their vocal passion for your brand earns them the right to some special treatment and inside knowledge. Forgetting to do this can quickly erode the trust you have built up.

6. **Invite them to become official (selectively).**

This step should be treated with caution, because it is not for everyone. In many cases, the power of accidental spokespeople is that they are marketing your brand without being motivated by any sense of obligation or promise of financial reward. If they were being rewarded or somehow incentivized, this could dilute their passion or their credibility. There are, however, select cases in which a passionate enthusiast may be the ideal individual to bring into your team as a more official part of it. This is what Moleskine did with Armand Frasco (see Chapter 2), and it worked.

7. **Create a program to foster more of them.**

This focuses very much on finding accidental spokespeople who are already out there and embracing them. The last point to mention, though, is that sometimes these accidental spokespeople can come from deliberate efforts to foster them. This could be in the form of a contest to find passionate brand believers, or bringing out the potential accidental spokespeople from loyalty programs you are already running for customers. The point is, once you become adept at finding and embracing your accidental spokespeople, the next step is to find a better way of encouraging more.

How to Empower Your Employees

1. **Kill your employee-silencing policy.**

In Chapter 2, we learned about the common employee-silencing policy and how it has worked to keep accidental voices from emerging within an organization. The first step in empowering your employees to demonstrate more personality is to remove the stranglehold you have on them by not allowing them to talk publicly. Does this mean that every employee should be pushed toward the media for interviews? Certainly not. But the ideal method for doing this is to give employees reasonable guidelines for their personal interactions. A few basic elements of your *new* policy should be:

- Never pretend to be someone you are not or try to obscure your affiliation.
- Do not talk about secret company matters that might give our competitors too much information.
- Try not to represent yourself as an official spokesperson for our company if you are not.
- Be honest and do not lie or intentionally mislead people.

Don't be surprised if these four tenets become your *entire* policy.

2. Minimize escalation.

Everyone hates the moment when someone says they need to "escalate" something to a manager higher up on the corporate food chain. Customers hate it, because it usually means that they have spent the time up until the point of escalation talking to the wrong person who has no power to do anything. Employees hate it because it puts them in a situation of not having any real control to resolve issues for customers. Managers hate it because it means that they need to serve as the bad guys for every issue, large or small. The ideal of escalation is a plague, which is why you need to get rid of it. One idea is to do what Tim Ferriss, author of *The 4-Hour Workweek* (and master of personal efficiency), did—offer your employees full rein to fix any problem that can be resolved for $20 or less (or another amount reasonable for your business).

3. Reward them on the right metrics.

Many times empowering your employees means rewarding them because of the right reasons instead of the wrong ones. For example, Dell learned that by rewarding its call center staff based on speed of resolution, the company was actually unintentionally encouraging its call center teams to quickly transfer customers from one person to the next without resolving any issues. Anyone who has had to submit a budget for an annual event at a company knows that if you end up coming in under budget, your "reward" will be getting a lower budget next year. The incentive is to spend everything in your budget, regardless of whether you waste money or not. Every team learns behaviors that are rewarded and those that aren't. If you want your employees to become more individualistic, then you need to find the right rewards system to make it happen.

How to Create a Successful Company Blog[1]

1. **Decide whether you need a blog.**

   Blogging is not right for every business. This is not a piece of advice that you tend to hear often from the many blogging books out there. Each positions blogging as the ideal way to have a voice, get to know your customers, build relationships, and perhaps even save the world in the process. The fact is, blogging is not right for every organization. To find out if it's right for you, you need to be able to answer yes to the following qualifying questions.

   a. Can you make management of the blog officially part of someone's job responsibilities? (A blog won't work if there is no single person with ultimate responsibility for making it a success.)

   b. Are there members of your team who are excited about blogging? (Every successful blog is built upon contributors who

[1] For lots more resources on successful blogging, visit http://www.personalitynotincluded.com/bloggingadvice.

are passionate about it. Without that you just have something that people are forced to do, which usually fails.)

c. Can you create useful or interesting content beyond product stories or branded information? (The best blogs have content that goes beyond the narrow scope of product or brand information.)

d. Are you able to commit the time required to keep the blog up-to-date? (Blogs are relatively easy to start, but much more difficult to keep going.)

The first step in creating a successful blog is answering these four questions positively.

2. **Set up what you will measure.**

As you are setting up your blog, it is also important to understand what you are measuring and what the aim of the blog is. There are product-centric blogs that feature the latest deals and whose objective is to generate real sales from the blog. Other blogs are meant to give you an inside look at a company or help to humanize it. Blogs can also help build awareness of your organization or some key thought leaders within it. At a later stage, being clear about a particular direction and intention for the blog will help you to judge whether it is working.

3. **Find the right voice(s).**

Identifying the right person or people within your organization to become bloggers can be the most difficult element of creating a successful blog, because the default reaction of many people within an organization is apprehension about whether they would have enough time to blog, and whether they could consistently create compelling enough content. The following are a few principles that can help you identify the right voice(s) for your blog from within your organization.

a. Think outside the CEO and senior members. Typically, the higher in rank an individual from your company is, the more reluctant she or he is to spend time on something like a blog. These senior managers often need to unlearn many years of experience in conversing in a different way.

b. Separate writing ability from speaking ability. One of the great myths that brands often fall for is that the same people who talk to the media will also be effective writing for a blog. Often, the perfect blogger for your organization is also the most unexpected.

4. **Create a schedule.**

In order to publish new content, it helps to develop a target for blogging of how many times per week the contributors will add something. This helps to set expectations and also ensures that your blog is kept timely. The best way to do this is to think about the blog as if it were any other media channel. Creating things like an editorial calendar, list of topics, and deadlines to post can all keep the blog content on track.

5. **Promote your content.**

There is an emerging method for promoting online content called *social media optimization,* which essentially refers to a way of optimizing your content so that it can more easily travel from person to person. It is a concept I first wrote about on my blog back in 2006, and it has since evolved into a specific practice that many marketing teams use to help their content get passed from person to person and be more easily shareable. It involves five basic elements.

a. **Increase your linkability.** Update your content frequently, create useful posts that people will save, and return to and make sure you use permanent links for each post (permalinks).

b. **Make tagging and bookmarking easy.** Add quick buttons to allow people to save your posts online more easily and tag your content with appropriate keywords that others can use as well.

c. **Reward inbound links.** Provide an incentive for people to link to your content and to increase the number of these links (an important standard for search engine rankings).

d. **Help your content travel.** Make your content as portable as possible by also using static files such as PDFs and submitting your content to relevant sites online.

e. **Encourage the mashup.** Be open about letting others use your content (as long they provide attribution), and syndicate your content through RSS to make it easy for others to build on it.

6. **Forge relationships with bloggers.**

   A key benefit of having a blog is the ability to forge new relationships with bloggers. Think of having a blog and consistently contributing to it as a way that you can start to understand other bloggers from the inside out. If your business is already reaching out to bloggers to try to build relationships, this will make your efforts more informed. If you are not, then having your own blog and an authentic voice offers a boost to your credibility when you do decide to start contacting bloggers.

How to Hire Employees with Personality

I've discussed empowering employees and how to spot your accidental spokespeople among employees. Another natural subject to consider is how to actually hire employees who are most likely to remain individuals and naturally bring more personality to your brand through their uniqueness and authenticity.

1. **Use unconventional advertising.**

   The first step in hiring employees with personality is to think unconventionally about advertising new job openings. Placing an ad in a newspaper or online is an obvious method. Can you post a challenge in a social network online and see who solves it? What about sharing your need to expand your team to your customers and seeing if they can offer a referral or even if one of your customers might be interested in working for you.

2. **Think outside the role.**

   The best candidates I have ever hired have been people who came along who did not fit into one role in particular, but would obviously be an asset to the team. The greatest mistake you can make is to let someone like that go because there is no existing role that he or she would fit well within. Hiring is an opportunistic activity, so when you have an opportunity to hire a star, do it. You can always craft a role (or merge two existing ones) to accommodate that person's special talents at a later stage.

3. **Understand why they are leaving.**

   One of the best ways you can learn about someone's personality when hiring is by understanding why that person is leaving her or his previous role. As we have learned in this book, the majority of companies do not use their personality particularly well or encourage their employees to have voices. As a result, many people are seeking a new role in which they can be more of an individual, and you may find the ideal candidate ready to work in a role with personality.

4. **Ask leading interview questions that elicit personality.**

Forget about the silly type of personality-related questions asked at parties, like whether you consider yourself an extrovert or an introvert. Those only give you an idea of what kind of role candidates think they might fit into. Instead, ask questions that give you more insight into the personal characteristics of an individual. Positioning them in a common scenario with a customer and asking them how they might react is a good example.

Chapter 3 Guides & Tools

Deconstructing Personality: An Outline

Personality is the unique, authentic, and talkable soul of your brand that people can get passionate about.

THE ELEMENTS OF PERSONALITY[1]

Element	Deconstruction
Unique	Different from anything or anyone else
Authentic	Real, believable, and not fake
Talkable	Interesting, simple, and viral
Soul	Significant, honest, and not superficial
Brand	Product, service, company, or your own personal brand
People	Customers, partners, employees, and yourself
Passion	Loyal, vocal, and deep belief

[1] For a downloadable version, visit http://www.personalitynotincluded.com/deconstruction.

The UAT Filter: Quick Reference Chart

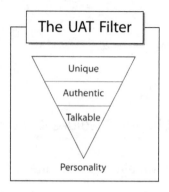

How to be unique	1. Find the uncontested space 2. Position yourself 3. Create a twist 4. Think outside your region
How to be authentic	1. Define a credible heritage 2. Demonstrate passion and belief 3. Foster individuals instead of people 4. Have motives beyond profit
How to be talkable	1. Offer something of value and limited 2. Have a hook that is shareable 3. Get out of the way

For a full description of the points mentioned is this table see pages 85–99 in Chapter 3.

Chapter 4 Guides & Tools

The Primary Backstory Picker

In Chapter 4, we learned about the different types of backstories that companies can use, and how they can do it effectively in order to offer a credible heritage that their customers can believe in. The guide below offers some more detail on how to pick the story that would serve best as the primary story for your business. This backstory is not meant to serve as the complete description of your business, but to offer you a starting point. The other story models can work as secondary narratives backing up the primary one.

Backstory Type	Common Industries	Use It as Your Primary Story If ...
The Passionate Enthusiast	• Niche retail • Social networks • Family businesses	Your business could be described as a labor of love, your founders are experts in your industry, and your business has grown mainly through word of mouth.

Backstory Type	Common Industries	Use It as Your Primary Story If ...
The Inspired Inventor	• Technology/ electronics • Pharmaceutical • Fashion	Your business is based on a new invention different enough from the rest of the world to be considered "inspired" (and is most likely patented).
The Smart Listener	• Food and CPG • Travel • Consulting	Your business was founded as the result of listening to customers, partners, or others and continues to rely on customer opinions to evolve.
The Likeable Hero	• Nonprofits/ advocacy • Health care • Green/ environmental	Your business was started by an individual with a big idea to do something to change the world and could reasonably be called a "hero."

Backstory Type	Common Industries	Use It as Your Primary Story If ...
The Little Guy vs. Big Guy	• Food/dining • Travel • Retail • Any industry with dominant players	Your business has a product or service that is designed to take on the dominant competitor (preferably faceless) in an industry and succeed in part based on its role as an "underdog.

Creating the "Passionate Enthusiast" Backstory

To learn about this story model and examples of brands that use it, turn to page 114.

To see when it may be the right story model for your brand, use the backstory picker on page 113.

THE PASSIONATE ENTHUSIAST BACKSTORY: A driven individual takes a personal passion and builds it into a successful business.

Characters	Establish the expertise and passion of the founders for the business by sharing stories of their credentials and stories of how and why they are enthusiasts.

Challenge	Describe how other enthusiasts need what your company offers and why no other enthusiasts have been able to do it in the same way that your organization has.
Vision	Outline the bold idea and vision of your business and how it offers a product or service for other enthusiasts that they have wanted, but not had until now.
Conflict	Share the arguments of the naysayers who did not believe in the idea and why they felt that way.
Triumph	Return your focus to today, and demonstrate how your business connects with other enthusiasts and succeeds based on word of mouth.

Elements of the "Inspired Inventor" Backstory

To learn about this story model and examples of brands that use it, turn to page 117.

To see when it may be the right story model for your brand, use the backstory picker on page 113.

THE INSPIRED INVENTOR BACKSTORY: A tireless inventor creates
something new and different by not giving up on his or her vision.

Characters	Associate the common qualities of inventors (perseverance, passion, creativity) with the individuals working at your business and the original founders.
Challenge	Talk about the industry you are in and the barriers that have existed before now in relation to smart invention, and how true inspiration has been difficult to achieve in the past.
Vision	In this story, the vision is crucial because it describes what was "inspired" about the inventors' process.
Conflict	With every great invention, something always stands in the way. Whether it is people or the process of getting it to market, the conflict is the story of the struggle to overcome the mishaps and barriers that almost killed the invention.

Triumph	The triumph, of course, is the invention itself and how it becomes successful as others discover it and the inventors realize their dreams.

Note: Though this story uses the term "inventor," you should not think of it solely as describing product inventions. An inspired inventor can be a designer, an artist, a writer, or an architect. The point is that not every inspired inventor gets her start coding software in a garage or blowing off his eyebrows in a lab.

Elements of the "Smart Listener" Backstory

To learn about this story model and examples of brands that use it, turn to page 121.

To see when it may be the right story model for your brand, use the backstory picker on page 113.

THE SMART LISTENER BACKSTORY: A new company is created as a result of listening to customers, partners, or others.

Characters	Smart listening and innovation based on it can come from anyone. Because of this, setting up the characters for this type of backstory means also establishing that your corporate culture is one that values listening and acts on it.

Challenge	The key challenge that smart listening companies face is that there can be many barriers to acting on knowledge gained from smart listening, particularly at a time when many businesses demand analytics, or feasibility analysis, or other scientific methods of confirming what is learned through listening.
Vision	The vision in your story comes from a select group of individuals who believe in doing what they hear your customers asking for and having a way to do it that they know can satisfy people who want it.
Conflict	Overcoming the more analytical minds and taking a risk on an idea that is largely based on what some people may consider "a hunch" is a big step and is usually the central conflict to be navigated in a Smart Listener backstory.
Triumph	The triumph is when the listening pays off and the product or service that was launched turns out to be exactly what the customers were asking for. The added benefit is that this triumph usually makes naysayers and other companies look foolish for not doing it themselves or supporting it.

Elements of the "Likeable Hero" Backstory

To learn about this story model and examples of brands that use it, turn to page 123.

To see when it may be the right story model for your brand, use the backstory picker on page 113.

THE LIKEABLE HERO BACKSTORY: A dedicated individual overcomes all odds to make his or her idea work.

Characters	The character behind the Likeable Hero backstory is the most crucial element as the story is usually based on the vision of that person. It needs to be someone who has motives beyond profit and who could reasonably be considered a "hero."
Challenge	A hero usually has a big challenge to face, and it is not related to competition. The challenge in this type of story is some sort of crisis or issue that needs to be solved. It could be something as big as global poverty, or something as personal as a rebirth of individual faith.
Vision	The vision of the likeable hero is to transform people and lives in some way through what their organization does.

Conflict	The most common obstacles of this type of story are people who do not believe in the mission or doubt that it can succeed.
Triumph	The triumph is in the likeable hero persevering and building a successful business that people can get passionate about. The idea discussed earlier in the "Techniques" section of this book about karmic marketing can also factor into this type of backstory.

Elements of the "Little Guy vs. Big Guy" Backstory

To learn about this story model and examples of brands that use it, turn to page 125.

To see when it may be the right story model for your brand, use the backstory picker on page 113.

THE LITTLE GUY VS. BIG GUY BACKSTORY: An underdog company takes on a seemingly unbeatable big adversary.

Characters	The main character in this story is a founder with courage and the drive to take on a big competitor that has dominated a field and seems unbeatable.

Challenge	This element is relatively obvious, a large competitor that virtually owns an industry or type of product is the adversary in your story and presents the most significant challenge.
Vision	Ultimately, it is the vision that your business can succeed despite going against the big guys that makes this story work. The vision should define what makes your business different and better than the big guys you are taking on and why your business deserves to grow.
Conflict	Having a big established industry player against the new little guy is one of the oldest storytelling conflicts. In your back-story, this conflict usually leads to the increase in popularity of your business.
Triumph	Triumph does not mean overtaking the big guys. In most cases, that doesn't happen. Instead, the triumph of the little guy is to be able to capture enough market share from the big guys to cause them to worry, and to create a niche for your business that your bigger rivals are unable to contest.

Buzzword Bingo

Ban the Buzzwords

the only thing seperating him from oblivion was a thin, porous membrane of second-rate buzzwords.

(c)gapingvoid.com

As part of the writing of this book, I issued an open call online for people to share their favorite examples of buzzwords. The query received many responses, which are compiled into the ultimate Buzzword Bingo game. Of course, Buzzword Bingo is most fun when you have others to play along. Download the full printable sheet online at:
www.personalitynotincluded.com/bingo.

Chapter 5 Guides & Tools

How to Build Your Authority

In order to effectively fight the barriers to using personality in your organization, as I shared earlier in the book, you first need to build your authority. The power of this authority will not be based on role, title, or pay grade, but on something far more fundamental and enduring—respect. *Building your authority is all about earning respect.* Respect is the currency that allows you to gain support for anything you propose and to inspire others to believe in you. So how can you go about building your authority?

1.   **Value other opinions.**

     The first rule for earning respect from anyone is to offer them your respect. You have to give respect to get respect, as the popular saying goes. Valuing the opinions and beliefs of others, even when they differ from your own, is a central element in creating this mutual respect. When you value others' opinions, it also means that you must actively listen to them. And when someone feels that you have heard what they said and valued it, this will build their trust in your humanity and judgment and a feeling that their interaction with you was a positive one.

2. Speak second (or last).

One of the most important, and most neglected, keys to building authority is the practice of listening first and talking second. What this allows you to do is hear other points of view before you begin to speak. Then you will be able to address in a meaningful and focused way any opposing views that have been expressed. This is not the same as half listening to what someone is saying while you compose your response in your head. Rather, it is about addressing the main points that someone else has made and using your position as second (or last) speaker to demonstrate that you were listening to other points of view while you make your own comments.

3. Offer a point of view.

Having a deliberate point of view is a necessity when it comes to building your authority. This means that you should have convincing reasons for doing what you do and question the things that you believe are wrong, and should stick to your views. This doesn't mean you should be inflexible; after all, it is possible to be completely right, and meet someone with an opposing point of view who is also completely right. Respect also grows during situations in which you were determined and even vocal about a particular point of view and argued it convincingly, whether your point of view prevailed or not.

4. Avoid condescension.

In Chapter 5, I talked about the in"duh"viduals about whom Scott Adams often writes in his *Dilbert* cartoons. Right now, making fun of your coworkers and their relative lack of intelligence in comparison with your own is a popular ploy in the marketing, media, and entertainment industries. The wild popularity of *The Office* in the United States (and the original in the UK) stems from this belief that we are all working with maladjusted, neolithic idiots who have no social skills. The challenge while working among all this negativity toward coworkers is to find a way to avoid being condescending toward peers who may not always follow what you are trying to do. If you can do it, however, you will stand apart from most of the other people in your office and gain the loyalty of these misunderstood coworkers.

5. **Share the credit.**

   Nothing fosters respect more than bringing others into the successes you may enjoy within an organization. As long as someone made a contribution to some project of yours that was successful and for which you are receiving some type of praise, it is always a good policy to find a way to share that credit with a wider team (including particularly any junior or "backoffice" staff, who do not usually get to enjoy such compliments).

6. **Have a personal brand.**

   This final point is a crucial one, but also one that has far more importance to your authority and the rest of your career than a simple list-item in one guide. If you purchased this book from one of my "special" partners, then you already have everything you need to know to build your personal brand. For the rest of you, I'll just leave you a clue as to how you can get it as well.[1]

---

[1] http://www.personalitynotincluded.com/pbe (for the password, use "brandyou").

How to Sell Personality to Your Boss

1. **Prove that it matters.**

    Before you can get your business or your boss to agree to focus on personality, you have to find a way to prove that it matters. One of the most powerful ways to do this is to demonstrate the penalties a business can suffer for not having a personality. Such faceless organizations have weak or nonexistent relationships with their customers, suffer low loyalty from both customers and employees, experience negative brand perception by the public, and have a host of other deficiencies. On the other hand, as many stories throughout this book attest, there are numerous brands that are using personality to build more positive customer relationships and to stand out from their competitors. In many of those cases, personality is the factor that makes the greatest difference.

2. **Associate with key concerns.**

    Personality is closely linked with business topics that are getting a lot of attention today. Word-of-mouth marketing, social media and blogging, and authenticity in business are all hot topics. Associating the need for personality with some of these key concerns, which your boss may already be aware of, is a good way of defining why you need to focus on this element as well.

3. **Highlight missed opportunities.**

    In Chapter 6, we focused on identifying personality moments and learned that many of the best opportunities to demonstrate your personality come in the everyday interactions you have with your customers rather than during the customer "acquisition" phase that most brands spend the majority of their time and money on. Cataloging some of these moments in your own business and demonstrating to your boss the opportunity to capitalize on them for relatively low cost is a great way to illustrate the times when personality could be injected into your current interactions with customers.

4. Use competition for pressure.

It is no surprise that the most undeniable motivating force is often what competitors are doing. If you can research and find instances of your competitors using personality effectively to connect with their customers, this can provide great fodder for you to share with your boss to incentivize her or him to begin to better incorporate personality into your business, or risk being left behind by your competitors.

5. Start small.

Just as with any sale, the process of learning to use more personality needs to feel like an incremental and achievable task for your business to accomplish over the long haul, rather than an instant overhaul. To this effect, it is important to let your boss know that there are ways of starting small. Perhaps your first step would be to conduct searches to find your accidental spokespeople, or to craft a new history of your company that uses some of the lessons of the backstory. Either way, the point is to demonstrate that there is a way of doing small things that can add up to big results.

How to Conquer the Success Barrier

1. **Understand that current success does not extend infinitely.**
    The hardest message to sell within a successful organization is that just because the method you are communicating today seems to be working, this doesn't mean that it will work tomorrow. The only way to demonstrate that this is true is by offering up a relevant example of another business that stayed the course in the same way you believe your business is doing—and how it ended unfavorably.

2. **Listen to what your customers are not telling you.**
    As I shared in Chapter 5, the most dangerous thing you can have sometimes is satisfied customers, because they rarely complain or tell you what needs to be improved. Here are a few ways to listen to what your customers are not telling you.

    a. **Read deeper into your Web stats.** Most organizations look at topline results from their Web stats to understand overall traffic levels, clicks, and little else. More meaningful stats could include a drop in usage of a "send to a friend" feature (meaning your audience is sharing the site with fewer others), or fewer visits to your site from a direct URL as opposed to a link (indicating fewer people are hearing about your site directly and typing in the URL versus using search).

    b. **Monitor online conversations.** I have talked about this idea several times throughout the book as a core concern that brands should have. Monitoring what people are saying about your brand online can offer key insights into what they really think about you but may not be sharing directly.

c. **Create an outlet where employees can share conversations.** As we discussed in Chapter 2, your employees are already having conversations with others about your company and in many cases they are in the best position to hear what others are saying about you as well. To capture this knowledge, you need a way of asking your employees to share it. This could be something as simple as an anonymous "rumor box" into which employees put notes describing things they have heard, or some sort of employee survey or ongoing site where they can also enter this type of hearsay.

3. **Know where the next threat is coming from.**

Since the success barrier is so often caused by a lack of understanding of the newer competition that may threaten a currently successful business, knowing who is up-and-coming is crucial. This may require creating a list of new competitors to be published internally on a regular basis, and reading or consuming media that can highlight these threats.

4. **Think like your competitor.**

One of the best ways to get ready to conquer the success barrier is to find a way to think like your competitors by targeting your own business. If you are really successful at what you are doing, there is bound to be another company or individual targeting your success. Starting to think like that business can help you prepare for the upcoming challenges and inspire you to take action sooner rather than later.

5. **Start with optimization.**

When it is succeeding, any organization will be reluctant to abandon methods it feels are working for those that are untried. For that reason, the easiest path to change is to describe any new thinking as a method for optimizing what you are currently doing (whether it is or isn't doesn't really matter). Once you do this, you are using the type of language that is unlikely to be ignored or dismissed because it has an easy to understand point of reference. Do this, and you will be in a position to overcome the success barrier.

How to Conquer the Uncertainty Barrier

1. **Outline the consequences of action versus inaction.**

Uncertainty means not knowing what is going to happen. Many organizations equate this with losing control and are therefore reluctant to use personality or change the way they have communicated in the past. The main reason for this is that uncertainty causes you to focus on the consequences of action. If we do this, what are the worst things that could happen? This is the first mode of thinking that you need to change, by encouraging people to think proactively about what could happen to your brand if you do nothing. This may seem a bit like painting a picture of fear, but it is not about sensationalizing the consequences. The point is just to change the conversation from focusing on the risks of acting to the risks of not acting.

2. **Reduce the penalty for mistakes.**

    Once you have a list to start with, you need to find a way to reduce the penalty for making a mistake. I shared in Chapter 5 the example of the GPS system and how it made experimenting with new ways of getting from one point to another much less stressful because it reduces the "time cost" of making a wrong turn. You need to do the same thing so that you can encourage your team to get past the uncertainty barrier they may be holding on to.

3. **Collect and share knowledge.**

    Knowledge is the surest way to combat the uncertainty barrier, because it can make uncertainty irrelevant. To use knowledge, you can consider sharing stories of businesses that have managed to use their personality more effectively and how easily these efforts could be translated to your business. This book should offer a good place to start, with many of the stories used in this book offering you a starting point. You can also outline the ways that your business can more effectively connect with its accidental spokespeople, or use its personality moments. The more easily understandable these efforts are, the more likely it is that you can get buy-in from your organization to do them.

4. **Embrace smart risks.**

    The last stage in conquering the barrier of uncertainty is to focus on an area you might call smart risks. These are opportunities that are a bit risky, but represent risks worth taking because the downside is so low. Examples of these types of opportunities include reaching out to customers who have been vocal about how much they love your business and want to be more involved in it or help you with it. Or perhaps there is a close circle of trusted friends and advisors that could be part of an effort to add a human element to your business. These are all smart risks because they already have some connection to your brand and you are simply finding ways to best use that.

How to Conquer the Tradition Barrier

1. **Determine why tradition is important.**

    Few people would argue that tradition in many companies takes on an almost supreme level of importance, but understanding why is not something that most employees are used to doing. The problem with tradition is that it has become a concept that most people accept without thinking about. An obvious danger with this is that tradition can be illogical, outdated, and in many cases can be the main barrier that stands in the way of more effectively using personality in your marketing. The first step in combating this barrier is to understand which of two key areas it comes from.

    a. **Nostalgia**—This is the first and most common reason why tradition is accepted in organizations. It is usually accompanied by the description of this being the way that a company has "always done it," which is based on an outdated series of actions or ways of thinking that early members of a company first pioneered.

    b. **Success**—A much more powerful argument for tradition, this is an argument for a way of doing things that is based on it having actually worked in the past. If this is the type of tradition your organization has, refer to the guide on conquering the success barrier, above, as this will be more relevant for you.

2.   Accept that you must keep it.

Once you have established that you are dealing with a tradition based in nostalgia, it makes your job far easier. More than any other type of barrier, thinking about "conquering" it will likely not work. The reason is that traditions based on nostalgia are powerful things and die very rarely within companies. Think about any example you can of a company that had a deeply embedded tradition and where any employee or manager who comes out against it is usually reviled or considered to not understand the culture of the company. The best way to deal with a barrier of tradition is to find a way to keep it while still minimizing the barriers it raises.

3.   Learn to add to it rather than replace it.

Once you have accepted that traditions based on nostalgia die hard, you are ready to work with it. Similar to dealing with the success barrier, you need to think in terms of optimization in order to most effectively deal with this barrier.

How to Conquer the Precedent Barrier

1.   Find a point of reference.

In an organization that always requires a precedent, the only way to sell a new idea is to find a point of reference. Luckily, no matter what you are trying to do, there will always be something someone has already done that can be used as a precedent.

This does not mean, however, that you need to copy an idea that someone else has already used. What it does mean is that you need to find something I call a "halfway precedent."

2. **Use it as a halfway precedent.**

A halfway precedent is a precedent in a campaign that another company has undertaken or a marketing strategy it has used with a single element that could be similar to what you are trying to do with your company. This element might be the way the other company describes its backstory, or it might take a similar approach to embracing its accidental spokespersons. Whatever the hook, finding the right examples from another company to use as a halfway precedent can help you to combat the precedent barrier.

3. **Demonstrate how you are the "same, but different."**

If you have spent any time in Thailand, you will recognize this phrase as a common way of describing how two things can be almost the same, and yet be different. The point of the halfway precedent is that you can satisfy the people in your organization who require some kind of precedent in order to believe in an idea, but still do something different and untried. Something that is the same same but different.

Chapter 6 Guides & Tools

AN INDEX OF PERSONALITY MOMENTS

The table below should give you an idea of the kinds of opportunities for personality moments that can come out of each phase of the buying cycle. It offers a few example situations that you may find useful depending on the type of business you are in.

Phase of Buying Cycle	Common Actions (depending on your business)
Researching Looking for information on what to buy	• Searching for information • Ordering product literature • Reading reviews online or talking to others • Asking for advice

Phase of Buying Cycle	Common Actions (depending on your business)
Purchasing Deciding to buy and completing the process	• Waiting in line to order or purchase • Placing an order and receiving confirmation • Paying for a product or service • Getting to and from a retail destination (travel)
Interacting Receiving what you bought and using it	• Receiving a product • Unpacking, learning, reading, or using it • Returning or exchanging items
Sharing Telling someone about your purchase or sending complaints or compliments	• Telling someone about your experience • Recommending or referring the product • Sharing negative opinions with others about the product • Writing a review or blog post online

Bibliography Not Included

I hate bibliographies. Chances are, if you ever took any courses in school which required you to use the same archaic format with commas, semi-colons and underlines, you know why I feel like I do. Still, in writing a book, a standard element is a list of sources that I used while writing the book. Throughout *PNI*, I used footnotes to indicate sources, however these cannot replace a full listing of resources. As you can imagine, many of them were online and printing the URLs here would simply require you to retype long URLs or indecipherable strings of characters in order to get to them.

Rather than force you to do that, I have created a unique style of bibliography as a companion to this book that you can access by going online to www.personalitynotincluded.com/resources.

On this page, you will get not only a full list of links to resources used in this book, you can also browse them by keyword, click on them directly to read articles or purchase books, and even get a printable list of resources and links (just in case you really want to have a hardcopy version that you can carry with you).

A Note on Research

Or How to Claim a Vacuum Cleaner on Your Tax Return

Research can be a scary thing. Some authors spend years doing it in preparation for writing a book that is designed to be as bulletproof as possible. Research is the armor that authors use to try to make everything they write incontestable. That is not my goal. If you happen to believe that research is what gives a book like mine credibility, then you should know that everything you read here was based on two simple techniques for doing research.

1. **Conversing.** In most cases where you see a story of a brand or individual highlighted, it is based on a direct conversation I had with someone. In a book that is partly about authenticity, there is no better way to gather the stories than to talk to real people. Along the way, many new examples emerged, I built new relationships with the people and brands profiled in this book, and the stories took on a new life.

2. **Consuming.** Truly understanding many brands is the result of doing more than just talking to people or finding content online. You have to buy and use the products. Hence the secondary title for this section. Yes, I did buy a Dyson and a Bugaboo. I joined Storyteller Coffee. I stayed at a Personality Hotel. Just about everywhere you see an example of a brand or an individual profiled in *PNI*, there is a real experience behind it.

So when I approached the task of doing research for *PNI*, I did not tackle it by digging up scholarly articles or traveling to far-flung places. I didn't enlist the help of a dozen enterprising young college students to join an exhaustive research team. I relied on the initial research of two smart marketers (who you can read more about on page 297), and just started talking to people and experiencing brands as a customer. It is what I would call the most important kind of research.

Bonus Content
Direct URLs Mentioned in *PNI*

For those of you who have been reading closely, you might have noticed lots of URLs that I mentioned throughout the book which point you online to get extended content or resources that relate to particular elements of the book. For ease, here they are in a single reference list:

- personalitynotincluded.com/bingo—Downloadable Buzzword Bingo Game
- personalitynotincluded.com/blog—The Personality Matters Blog
- personalitynotincluded.com/bloggingadvice—Links to resources on blogging
- personalitynotincluded.com/mp—Master of Personality Degree
- personalitynotincluded.com/pbe (for the password, use "brandyou")—Personality Not Included: The Personal Branding Edition
- personalitynotincluded.com/resources—Additional Resources
- personalitynotincluded.com/reviews—Full list of reviews and endorsements for *PNI*
- personalitynotincluded.com/techniques—Downloadable Bonus Techniques

For even more content, visit www.personalitynotincluded.com.

Index

Acknowledgments

The first and most obvious people I need to thank for *PNI* are all the faceless organizations and the people stuck working for them that made a book like this necessary. It is my sincere hope that I managed to offer a reason and a road map for them to change. To do that, throughout writing this book, I asked many people to talk to me about the topic of personality and how it related to their business. The ultimate acknowledgment I could offer to any of them was to put them in the book, and I did for many of them, so I won't repeat them here.

There are, however, two people who worked tirelessly to help me pull everything together and deserve my first thanks. Jinal Shah and Geeta Saini are two rising marketing stars who took on the huge task of helping to sift through stories, collect interviews, conduct research, and pull a story-driven book like this together. They are also dedicating their time, creativity, and passion to the marketing and promotion of *PNI*. Much of the credit for the stories that bring this book to life, as well as the marketing behind distributing it, goes to both of them.

To make the time to write this book, I also asked for the ultimate favor from all my colleagues in the 360 Digital Influence team at Ogilvy, to help cover work for me while I was out writing every Friday for more than four months. For that reason, a big thanks goes to John, Steve, Rachel,

Alison, Brian, Sara, Veronica, Kaitlyn, Qui, Laura, Robert (both of you), Wyatt, Mike, Kristin, Samantha, Aaron and Graham, as well as all my colleagues at Ogilvy PR who offered their understanding and helped to shift schedules around as I disappeared for a day each week. Most importantly, it was the support of two visionary leaders at Ogilvy—John Bell (head of 360 Digital Influence) and Marcia Silverman (CEO of Ogilvy PR) who let me evolve from blogger to accidental spokesperson to author while keeping my day job. Everyone should be lucky enough to work for people like them. As I move from having written the book into the marketing of it, I know I will owe many more thanks to colleagues who have already volunteered their time, contact lists, and expertise to help me promote it.

Looking backward for a moment, having an idea for a book and selling it are two very different things. I was fortunate last year at the SxSW show in Austin, Texas, to finally connect with Tim Ferriss, and I have him to thank for many early successes of my book, including connecting with my brilliant agent, Steve Hanselman, and, more important, for demonstrating to the publishing industry that a bestseller can be created through nontraditional marketing. The success of Tim's *The 4-Hour Work-week* was the precedent that let me try a lot of new things in promoting and distributing this book—and probably opened the door for more aspiring writers than Tim realizes.

PNI would also not be where it is without the strong editorial support from Herb Schaffner and the ongoing thoughts and contributions from the rest of the McGraw-Hill team. There is a difference between publishing your own book and working with real professionals to help you do it. Some may wonder why someone who built an audience blogging and writing about social media chose to go with a "traditional" publishing house. If I had to choose over again, I would take the same route in writing and publishing *Personality Not Included*. I love working with people who know what they're doing.

Speaking of professional people, my single greatest source of inspiration for this book has been a group of individuals for whom I have the utmost respect even though there are many of them I have never met. Being a marketing blogger, I am part of a community of individuals who collectively share their wisdom openly, often and most uniquely, without expectation of compensation. There are far too many to name, so I will just share here a general word of appreciation for all the bloggers who have shared their thoughts, support, and intelligence with me. I learn from all of you each day, and this book would be meaningless without your influence. If this book offers me a reason and opportunity to meet more of you in person, I will be a better marketer for it.

This book was also brought to life thanks to the illustrations of one brilliant blogger in particular, Hugh Macleod of Gaping Void. Those who know him also know that he takes an open source approach to his cartoons, letting people republish them widely, which helps them spread virally. He is fond of saying that people don't buy art, but they do buy wine, which leads him to his partnership with Stormhoek wines from South Africa. If you liked the book and particularly the illustrations, check out Stormhoek wines at www.stormhoek.com, pick up some great wine, and support what Hugh does. The world could use more artists (and marketers) with his philosophy.

I also have to thank my family, and particularly my reading panel of Rahul, Emily, Pranu, Nupur, Gaurav, Rifat, Nidhi, and Sid who offered early feedback on the book and helped make it better. To Anil, who gave me my first marketing job, and to Sunil who still manages to teach me something new every time I talk to him. I have to say, you are both the best kind of big brothers anyone could hope for. To the rest of my family, thanks for your continual love and encouragement. It has made a big difference.

I want to say a special thanks to my parents. To my Mom for believing in this project (as well as most everything else I have ever tried), and to my Dad for paving the way to make me among the third generation of authors in our family after him and my grandfather.

To my wife Chhavi for her daily support in reading and commenting on the book, brainstorming for marketing, listening to my never-ending stream of ideas, as well as handling two little boys on her own while I disappeared to write or market the book.

Finally, to Rohan, who spent a part of every Friday afternoon banging on Daddy's office door just to remind me he was "not bothering me." One day when he is older he'll read this and realize those breaks were the best part of my day.

Meet the Author

Rohit Bhargava is one of the founding members of the 360 Digital Influence group at Ogilvy Public Relations, one of the world's largest communications agencies. Describing himself as a marketer in a PR agency, he believes that personality matters and that telling people you are marketing to them is a good thing. Before joining Ogilvy, Rohit was Executive Producer at Leo Burnett in Sydney, Australia.

For the majority of his career he has been a hired marketing expert offering creative thinking and new ideas, and has worked on developing marketing strategy for more than a hundred brands, including launching dozens of marketing programs for products, from breakfast cereal to laptops, and causes, from heart disease to world hunger.

Rohit also authors the top-rated Influential Marketing blog where he has written more than 500 posts and been featured in media worldwide, including *The Wall Street Journal*, *BrandWeek*, *Fast Company*, *The Globe & Mail* (Canada), *Marketing China* (China), and *AdWeek* (Australia). He respects the power of social media and is proud to be a blogger—but now that you are reading this, he plans to enjoy being introduced as an author from now on nonetheless.

Rohit lives in Washington, D.C., with his wife and two young sons. For more details about the author, including Rohit's full backstory and a calendar of upcoming events, visit www.aboutrohit.com.

The Fake Ending
Why Are You Still Here?

In a small handful of movies, the end credits are not actually the end of the movie. The most common gag is for one of the main characters to address the audience after the credits with some kind of question about why you're still watching. It's time to go home now, they usually say.

You've successfully completed this book and now you understand how to inject more personality into your brand. I hope, you will be able to take the lessons presented here and use them to make a change within your organization. So why are you still reading? For those of you who are, I suppose there is one more thing I can offer. Sometimes, in the world of business, it helps to have an official title and certification. In case you work in an environment where it's all about how many acronyms you can put after your name, here is one you'll be interested in,

www.personalitynotincluded.com/mp

On this page, you'll find everything you need in order to create your own certification for yourself as a *master of personality*. Call yourself an "MP" if you like, and even print out your own diploma online with your name on it for all to see. In case you happen to be in a country that has a parliamentary model, you may already know that MP is also a common abbreviation for a "member of Parliament." This is a good thing, because with the MP after your name people will either recognize you as a master of personality or mistakenly think you are a member of Parliament. Either way, you win.

Okay, now the book is really over. Thanks for reading.